To Jill

BLITZ KIDS

KENNETH BLACKBURN

Broadcast
BOOKS

Very best wishes
Ken Blackburn

Published by **Broadcast Books** 4 Cotham Vale, Bristol BS6 6HR in association with BBC Radio Bristol 1995.

Copyright 1995 Ken Blackburn.

The BBC Radio Bristol series, *Blitz Kids* was first broadcast in 1991, and then re-broadcast in the present extended form, in May 1995.

isbn : 1 874092 70 2

Cover illustration by John Blackburn

Text illustrations by John and Ken Blackburn.

Book and cover design by Edmund Crewe,
2 Cotham Vale, Bristol BS6 6HR

Printed by the Bath Press, Bath, Avon.

The authour, Ken Blackburn

KENNETH BLACKBURN

Born in the St. Paul's district of Bristol in 1935, Ken, alone with his older brother John, were evacuees to the South West of England during the Second World War. After the war he emigrated with his family to New Zealand. He has been a freelance actor and theatre director for thirty years and has played a wide range of characters in the theatre and for film and television. His recent TV and film roles have been:

Hank Blair in "White Fang"
Sir Bruce Warner in "Shortland St."
The Gharmer in "Betty's Bunch".

In 1974 he was honoured by the Polish government with the *Amicus Poloniae* award for fostering cultural relations between Poland and foreign countries. He has a renowned expertise in accents and dialects which has often been called on for film narrations and commercial voice-overs, and narrated the BLITZ KIDS series for BBC Radio Bristol.

Today he lives in Auckland, New Zealand with his wife Carolyn, where they share their two storey colonial villa with their four boxer dogs. BLITZ KIDS is his first book.

Gran and Aunty May

CHAPTER 1

I was born in the Bristol Royal Infirmary on the 2nd of April 1935 to Florence Elizabeth May Beachem and Albert Frank Beachem, and christened Kenneth. My brother John Francis had been born two years earlier at the same place.

I remember nothing at all of my father, though I note from the Somerset House copy of my Birth Certificate that he was labelled "Barman of Bristol". I've often wondered whether that was a prestigious position in the Bristol of 1935. Albert Frank Beachem made the decision to end his life in March 1937 and the close proximity to my birth has given me cause for thought over the years. I often asked the question, "How did Dad die?" The least plausible story my Mother came up with was that Dad was breaking up coal in the cellar and a piece flew up into his eye and that was how he died. Well... this satisfied me as a very young child, but later the inconsistencies began to creep in, and there were times when she assured me that he'd died of the flu. I think I was about thirty when the full truth was told.

My mother was a domestic worker at the time, also a frustrated nurse, schoolteacher and singer. She once sang at the Blackpool Tower.. and was a regular vocalist accompanying the recorded music at the local skating rink. But our family had a long heritage as working class Bristolians and there was no support for her ambitions from my grandmother, herself a professional domestic who'd been "in service" since she was nine years old. "Humph!... getting ideas above yor station my gurl" she'd say.

My gran was known by everyone as Granny Hudd and she lived at 39 Monk St. in St. Paul's with my Aunty May (a spinster, and older sister of Mum). Gran never wore anything but black I remember, but then, it was the most popular colour at the time, and my Aunty May smelt of tobacco. I discovered later that Aunty May had worked in the same room of a factory for fifty years of her life as a "Stripper"... That's the honest truth! She was in charge of a table at the Wills No.1 factory in Bedminster which made cigarettes, and for up to ten hours a day they stripped the tobacco leaves from their stems. They were known as the "Strippers" and over a period of fifty years my aunty worked from one end of the table, to end up in charge at the top. She died in the mid sixties of cancer. Never smoked a cigarette in her life. I can still see Aunty May, Gran and Monk St. very clearly in my mind. Standing at the end of the road where it meets Newfoundland Rd., it was the first building in Monk St; right on the corner was "Scapens" pub, where the entire street would gather in the evenings, and where we as children sat outside on broad sills or on the pavement, knowing that at intervals we would be handed a lemonade or bag of crisps out of the window. Those crisps always had a twist of blue paper containing salt inside the packet. There was a chance here too to make a few pennies, for as the evening wore on it became easier to persuade the customers to pay for a child's treble solo rendered through the open window. I was as heart broken as any adult when Scapens was devastated by incendiary bombs.

Although every house frontage was identical in Monk St. to me at the time, the next house along from Scapens was the posh one. I suppose the fact that it was occupied by a kindly old couple who kept it freshly painted, and whose back garden was tidy and well-gardened, made it seem a better house than all the others. Or maybe because my Gran

Monk Street

and Aunty May lived next door, which was never in the same state of pristine freshness, though a more vigorously scrubbed front doorstep would be hard to find... But you see, there was an absence of men, or fathers, in my early recollections. I remember only my Uncle Sam visiting occasionally at the house in Monk St. So there was never a man about the house to do the sort of everyday maintenance work required, and all the other houses seemed to have this! The frontage design of every house in the street was identical: the upper storey window directly above the lower, and a front door that opened right onto the pavement across the scrubbed wooden entrance step. They continued in a straight line flush with a three foot wide pavement to the end of the street. Here you came up against a grey stone wall, the top of which my seven year old fingers could just reach to get a grip. Heaving yourself up and taking the leather off your toe-caps in the process, you looked down into the River Frome, better known as "The Danny" to local kids. It had a great expanse of mud bank on either side, with a channel of water about six feet across in the middle. I can still remember being in tears on this wall when a big fellow of sixteen or so brought down a seagull with an air rifle and continued to fill it with pellets until the fluttering ceased totally.

If you walked along the Danny wall, you could look into the back gardens of the houses right down Monk St. Most of them had an Anderson Shelter – a type of air raid shelter made of corrugated iron sheets sunk into the ground, wherein you stood more chance of dying of pleurisy than of being bombed. It had a roof that was usually covered by some gardening effort, maybe flowers or vegetables. At one time, it was a special treat to sleep out in the shelter at night and pull carrots from the garden for a midnight feast, though at a later date it proved less fun to be confined to it for three days and four nights while Jerry flattened the city of Bristol.

When my mother took a basement Flat at 79 Ashley Rd. directly opposite St. Barnabas Church, my brother and I continued to attend Newfoundland Rd. school until the time of evacuation. My mother went to work at Temple Meads Station for the Great Western Railway. She worked alongside Italian P.O.W.'s loading, unloading and pushing railway trucks to and fro in the yards.

It was a happy time all in all, and certainly full of excitement. My brother and I, Dennis Jay and Snotty Fox (so called because of a persistent runny nose, but he was never offended by it) would attend all the local incendiary fires, unexploded bomb sites and any other scenes of devastation following a raid. We all had our coveted personal collections of shrapnel, military badges, bullets, shell cases etc. along with the customary marbles and cigarette cards of footballers. These were our units of currency to acquire the good things in life like sweets, chewing gum, comics... or a ride on yer bike! Road tar, which we often used, was a poor substitute for the continuing sweet flavour of real chewing gum. An envied owner would often lend it out for a few hours on a swap deal for comics, but never for keeps!

My collection of shrapnel, in a flat Capstan cigarette tin, boasted a very special piece that just everyone wanted to borrow, and certainly hold. It was the jagged shard of a German shell that put my Uncle Sam out of the war. He was invalided out after being hit in the right elbow, and this prize piece of metal he had given to me for my collection. It was like having a prize conker, and always swung the deal on any bartering that was needed. The only drawback to its ownership was the number of times my Uncle Sam needed to borrow it back, and regrettably it was on such an occasion that he borrowed my entire collection to impress the bar at Scapens, and left it with the publican when he weaved his way home.

It was that same night that Jerry chose to drop several sticks of incendiary bombs and high explosives around Newfoundland Rd. and Monk St. and as I said, I was as heart broken as any adult when Scapens pub was devastated, and my shrapnel went up... for the second time.

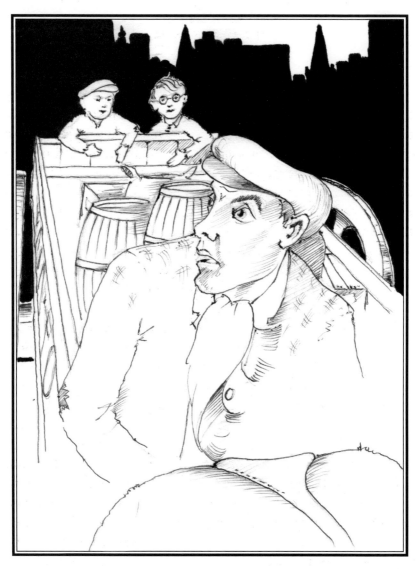

Woe betide if the driver saw you, that whip could reach right to the back.

CHAPTER 2

When Air Reich Marschall Goering started to become a little tetchy over the loss of so many German aircraft and more particularly for the unstoppable efforts of the R.A.F. in getting through to give Berlin such a pasting, he looked at a map of England and picked out the jewels in the crown for special treatment. These became known as the Baedaker Raids, after a very popular guide book of the times. Bristol was to be one of those jewels. Exeter was another, bombed in retaliation for the bombing of Essen. The well known features of Bristol that were blitzed included "Lennards Corner" which was a huge department store, the Triangle Cinema, the Coliseum dance hall and skating rink where Mum played the records and sang, the Bethesda Chapel on Brandon's Hill, Merchants Hall which had stood since the 1770's, the Seamen's Almshouses (also 18th century) and, very sadly, the "Prince's Theatre". The Docks at Hotwells and the Basin took a tremendous pounding, and all over the city there was a pox of craters, ruined football fields, and shattered buildings with their acrid smell of incineration. It always reminded me of kippers. When the vinegar factory went up there was a mouth-watering smell in the air for days. The sight of dolls houses with the roof off or with the side removed always reminds me of those days and nights on the streets of Bristol. The humour within the tragedy wasn't lost on me at the age of seven and eight either, because the most vivid memories are those which revealed the more private aspect of peoples lives when suddenly their homes would be "Open House" to the passing world. A free-standing wall with staircase attached and the scorched wallpaper still decorated with framed pictures hanging all askew. A top landing spring boarding into space. A fire still burning merrily in a second-floor grate of another house, halfway up a wall and no way of putting more coal on, unless you were thirty feet tall. Who was on the lavatory when the bomb hit, I wondered, because the chain was still swinging and the flush was going all the time!

There was a factory which we knew as the Marble Factory, though it actually produced bottles that had a marble in the neck, and when this was hit and the officials gone, it became something like King Solomon's Mines. We had a stakeout for excavation purposes, each jealously guarded and fortified and the process of recovering hundreds of clear marbles and Ginger Beer Stoppers went on for several weeks. Claims only changed hands for highly prized shrapnel, badges or bundles of Hotspur or Champion comics. There were a couple of hours of this activity after school, then we would all tear off down the back streets to be home before dark and count or sort out the booty. After a tiring day a more leisurely way of getting home was to sneak off the pavement and catch hold of one of the many drays carrying vinegar barrels along Newfoundland Rd. Provided the driver didn't see you, you could travel quite a distance with your elbows up on the back edge and your feet clipping the tops of the cobblestones. Woe betide if he saw you though. That whip could reach right to the back, and most of them didn't mind using it. The leather and canvas bag of feed was always slung at the back until a pause in the day's work, when it would be slung over the horse's ears at the other end of the vehicle. The tasty, nut-like grain would often filter through the holes in our trouser pockets and my Gran would say, "Wha's all these bleed'n seeds doin' on my clean floor?" "I dunno Gran" we'd say. "Thee bist lyin" she'd say. "No, I baint Gran, honest". "Well, yers a clip round the ear jus' in case".

How my Gran escaped the war is a mystery to me. She simply ignored it. She certainly wouldn't leave the house and get into the Anderson Shelter at the bottom of the garden when an air raid siren went, she just went about her planned routine of cooking, ironing, cleaning and what was called "doing for other people" while Bristol blazed all around her. "That bleed'n 'itler" she'd mutter, "I wish 'e 'ad my feet". And she'd lace on her black boots and head off into the crackling night to pick up somebody's bundle of ironing. She might have made use of the other type of shelter had we been able to afford one. It was called a "Morrison Shelter" and it had all the appearance of an enormous rat-trap: a large table top of plate steel that sat in the middle of the room, and was caged around with steel mesh, with a small gate that gave entry on one side. My brother and I were to experience the use of one at a later time when we were evacuated to Exeter. "Whas thee think I am, runnin' out the 'ouse every time the siren goes, Gord bleedin imey! (which was her own version of Gor Blimey) I'm stoppin' put, I got things to do!"

So the Air Raid Wardens would often be banging at the door of 39 Monk St., shouting "Put that light out" as my Gran pressed on with her work in the greenish blue glow of the gas lamp filament. We had no electricity. It was essential to achieve a total blackout when Jerry was overhead, as the telltale lights of a populated area usually guaranteed a disgorgement of high explosives or incendiaries. None of which worried my Gran, mind you, in fact, if she hadn't been so busy she'd have gone over and dealt with Hitler on her own. Remember *Old Mother Riley* in those early films? That was my Gran.

It was in April 1941 that Bristol and Coventry copped it really badly, and King George V1 came down to look around and talk to the people. It didn't mean much to me then, except that I remember

"That bleedin' Hitler...I wish 'e 'ad my feet."

laughing when Granny Hudd lost her balance and fell forward when trying to curtsey to him. He talked to everyone and shook hands and made everyone feel a lot happier. He had one of those posh camel-hair coats and a peaked army hat (no crown) which was a surprise! And he stuttered a bit too. He seemed to be everybody's hero. Air-raid wardens were part of the Home Front Defence Corps, usually middle-aged men in blue boiler suits and a steel helmet that said A.R.P. The ubiquitous gas mask was shoulder-slung, and they carried either a large torch or a stirrup pump for small fires. I had many opportunities to see them in action, controlling crowds, administering first-aid and comforting the bereaved. I saw them too when their nerve gave out, as it did with one who joined us in a city shelter one night. He crouched in a corner and shook and the tears flowed freely. I'd never seen a man do that before. Some of these men saw more action than the younger ones at the front line, but they didn't wear the medals. They often worked all night during a raid and then continued without sleep through the day, desperately digging out the buried victims from their collapsed homes. They gave unsparingly of everything they could to keep up the morale at home.

Among the war's unsung heroes as far as I was personally concerned, was Mary. Mary was a W.A.A.F. who worked at a Balloon Barrage base situated in the woods very near to where John and I were later evacuated in Exeter. One of our jobs every weekend was to go into the woods with a handcart and collect firewood, and it was on one of these occasions that we met Mary. She would have been about eighteen, I suppose, and she saw in us an opportunity to give that little bit extra for the war effort. We were delighted to be the benefactors in this case because it meant following Mary back to the base and waiting outside the window of a large Nissen Hut until she passed out a plate of hot bacon, eggs and fried bread for each of us. This turned out to be a regular event during our time in Exeter, and I doubt you would have found two more willing evacuees to go out and collect firewood in the whole of England. Dear Mary... we could give her nothing in return and to this day we don't know what she risked to do that for us. She didn't wear any medals either, nor did we ever know who she really was.

The other heroes of my acquaintance were men who stood in the queue at the pictures. The line was always very long, but generally you didn't mind queues during the war because they became a way of life and most people joined them in order to find out what they were for when they got up to the front – soap, shoes, meat, fish or fags. But everyone knew when they were queuing for the pictures because the Commissionaire, dressed in a braided uniform and cap, walked up and down the line calling out the seat prices and what seats could be had. If you could afford the expensive seats you could leave the queue and go in. "Three in the Grand Circle at 2/6d; four stalls at a shilling; and I've got a pair in the gallery at threepence". There was a restriction on cinema attendance according to the certificate of the film. For instance, two films showing that were classified U or Universal Exhibition was available to any age, If an A and a U were showing together you could only attend in the company of an adult. When two A's were on you couldn't go at all unless you were an adult. In order to ensure that we didn't miss any of the latest popular films, we would seek out our adult requirement from the queue and boldly say: "Hey, will you take us in Mister, we got our own money!" The fact that they usually did, wouldn't let you pay and also bought you a Wall's ice-cream at intermission, place them among the heroes who didn't wear the medals.

Boys in the Anderson Shelter.

CHAPTER 3

"Three ha'porth of scrumps please!" I don't suppose one in ten million would know what you were talking about today, but you could hear it any night of the week in a crowded fish'n'chip shop back in Bristol during the war. Admittedly, most people were there to buy fish and chips, but there'd always be a grubby kid with the arse out of his trousers and cardboard in his shoes trying to get served with "three ha'porth of scrumps please". Scrumps were the floating debris of batter bubbles and burnt chip that was scooped off the surface of hot fat in the frying vats, and dumped alongside. What a treat wrapped in the Daily Mirror this was, and there was no charge for salt and vinegar. You could fold your cap around them and stuff them down your jersey for added heat insulation, then feed off them at leisure while creating an oil slick from your chest to your chin... I can taste them even now! Food and adequate heating seemed to be the priorities then. My brother John and I were living with Mum, Aunty May and Gran at Gran's house in Monk St. All the cooking was done on a large coal range in the parlour. It had lids, drawers, doors pushed and pulled, grates that dropped and vents that opened – all of which my Gran manipulated with the skill of an engine driver to cook up a meal. She also heated irons on it when clothes needed pressing, or tongs when hair needed curling.

The only food not prepared here was the Christmas pudding, and that was done in the copper out in the wash-house. The stove was the centre of our lives, and as befitting such a monument it was cleaned inside and out then blacked with a product that today has racial over tones. The mantelpiece above was fringed with a tasselled pale green velvet cloth crowned by pictures and tinned treasures surrounding the "News" and "I.T.M.A." – Bebe Daniels and Ben Lyon, and of course the "Andrews Sisters". Yes, the radio! At the apex of our lives it represented entertainment and information on the state of the war. At 9 o'clock each night nobody dared to speak for fear of missing some important item on the News.

A drawstring to the side of the stove raised and lowered the washing, which seemed ever present, and the hob was always occupied by damp clothes and bare feet being warmed beside wet boots. Keeping it fired brings back the two worst memories I have of my Gran, though only the first directly concerned the stove.

We had an old pram in the greenhouse. It was of the gracious carriage variety and it was big! Who knows, it was probably mine at an earlier age. It was brought out once a week for the collection of the coal. This particular exercise meant accompanying Gran on an excursion along the railway tracks, trying to push a large but quite well-sprung vehicle over uneven stones, sleepers and tracks, while picking up the coal nubs which had fallen from passing engines and their tenders. Though this may have been hard work, it didn't carry with it the embarrassment attached to the other occupation that the pram was used for. Around the corner from Monk St. and a short distance along Newfoundland Rd. there was a vinegar factory. This factory transported large barrels on open drays which were drawn by enormous Clydesdale horses. My Gran was a badly failed horticulturist, but she held an implicit belief in manure! So whenever a dray clopped its way down Monk St. my Gran would thrust the hearth shovel at me and instruct me to follow with the pram, and, God willing! I would come home with a reason-able steaming load for the garden and, God willing! not meet any of my friends on the way. It was a mortifying experience.

Collecting manure for Gran's garden.

Another memory of Gran involved the weekly trip that my brother and I had to make to collect the bread at Hotwells. I suppose it was a Church charity that supplied it. My very vivid memory is of a high green door with black studs that had to be knocked upon. When it opened, there was a long trestle table heavily laden with dark crusty loaves. Two of these were placed in our hands and we'd set off home again. Not all of the deliciously tempting fresh bread arrived of course – after all, you don't set pigs to guard your pantry. But I suppose the forbidding thought of Gran's anger ensured that we were very judicious about changing the shape of the loaf too much.

On one occasion I was sent alone to get the bread, and while I was returning from Hotwells, one of Jerry's daylight raids occurred. These were rare but effective. Taking all the short cuts I knew, and hugging the two loaves to my pounding chest, I ran hell for leather through back streets and bomb sites toward home. While clambering through the middle of one devastated bomb site, history decided to repeat itself, and with a deafening BANG! accompanied by a hail of bricks, plaster and pipes, I lost consciousness. How long I lay there, and how far from home I was, I don't know now. My only memory is of tears and a very bloody left foot with no shoe... and even more tragically, no bread! My Gran greeted me at the front door with the words: "Ne'er mind thy foot, wers the bleedin' bread?" Three bus loads of people were killed near College Green on that day in 1942.

Black bread and margarine seemed to grace most tables, and although the name conjures a sickening image, the bread so referred to was actually grey. It was something to do with the poor quality of the flour at the time.

The margarine was another story altogether. It certainly didn't have the flavour of today's substitute for butter, and even as I write my stomach revolts at the memory of this white paste with the taste of rubber. The only similar flavour I can relate it to is that experienced when trying to inflate the bladder of a football by mouth and having it blow back down your throat. Mind you, I will say that my revulsion for margarine was recognised at home and it was only while evacuated that the nightmare grew as I was compelled to force it down. Jam sandwiches was school lunch for me and John. You could get school dinners which were hot, but they were fourpence a week, and there were a lot more of us who couldn't afford that than could. I know Miss Fisk, our teacher, used to give us tea at lunchtime if you brought your own cup.

Newfoundland Rd. School was a ten-minute walk from Monk St. – if you went straight there and didn't divert over the bomb sites looking for shrapnel and souvenirs – and it was a two minute run home, where you quickly divested yourself of coat, cap and gas mask and got back out into the street where the real world was. Monk St was cobbled and had a gutter running down the centre of it which was great for matchstick races and regattas of Woodbine packets.

There we would be until the light was too dim to sail or my Gran chased us in to the scrubbed table for tea. "You bleedin' tykes'll be the death'o'me one day" she'd say. "C'mon our Flar! (my mother, whose name was Flo). "Wers our Mary Ann then?" And when Aunty May joined us we'd settle at the table for the evening meal.

My Aunty May was the most stable factor in the family. She had a job at Wills No. 1 factory in Bedminster, and she travelled to and fro every day. She was warm and cheery with a lap to match, and always arrived home with the Daily Mirror and sweets. She smelt strongly of tobacco, though not a smoker. It seems she almost got married once;

Aunty May washing her feet.

she was certainly engaged. The front room of 39 Monk St was like a sanctuary – though not a comforting one. Everything in it seemed to be entombed, and I looked in most often through the front window beside the front door. You could just see in, if the light was right, between the gap in the lace curtains and the whistling boy statue who guarded its secrets. It was a memorable day when Aunty May took me into the room, and one by one fondled and explained the engagement presents as she took them out of the glass-fronted bureau. There was even an early type of electric iron in its box. All were arranged on display – none was ever used. She died a spinster. Plagued throughout her working life by a persistent rash on her feet that was tobacco induced, she and Gran shared a soothing foot-bath every evening.

CHAPTER 4

Time has clouded the less relevant details, but it must have been mid 1942, because there were a large number of Italian prisoners of war at Temple Meads Station the day I was first evacuated from Bristol. My research on this has shown that 18,500 children were evacuated from the Bristol Elementary School. At the end of three months 9,500 had returned home.

I stood with my brother John on the main platform waiting to board the train for Weston-Super-Mare. We had one case between us, a luggage label pinned to our coats declaring names and destination, and each with our string slung cardboard boxed gas mask across the shoulder. From end to end, the platform was choked with emotional partings and not even a handful of free liquorice allsorts from the A.R.P. man could alleviate the misery.

John was two years braver than me and charged with the task of 'taking care of our Ken, saying Thank You to the lady, and writing home'. We were going to be very lucky too because Weston had a beach and a pier and it would be like having a holiday, so our Mum said, and she promised to visit as often as she could. Weston did have a beach, and when the tide was out you could hunt for pennies in the mud under the pier, but the rolls of barbed wire and the "Prohibited" notices placed the sand, and paddling, strictly out of bounds.

The lady, Mrs Sandford, lived in a semi-detached two-storey house in Southville Rd. with her husband. She was welcoming and kindly as she took in the five evacuees from Bristol – all boys, the eldest of us

Ready for the evacuation.

aged fifteen. Mr Sandford at half her height and a third her weight was further diminished by the loss of his right forearm in the First World War. The stump, covered by a sock and an elastic band, was a forbidding sight to a seven-year-old; and as time later proved, the fear was compounded by the many episodes that required one or other of us to keep at stump's length when he swung, in a foreshortened attempt to hit us with it. Perhaps he'd always been right-handed and had never come to terms with the disability in times of stress! Certainly a slap with the left hand would have been more effective in the short term, and less damaging to one's dreams in the long term. He kept a budgie in a cage for which he reserved a seldom-heard tone of affection. It became apparent that this bluefeathered tweeter was the sole recipient of caring in the household.

A daughter in the W.A.A.F's who worked at a balloon barrage base, and a son in his twenties who came and went often seemed to place a considerable strain on the bedroom accommodation, and within a short time the five of us evacuees accepted that we would be permanently sharing the same double bed in the upstairs front room. As the youngest and smallest, I occupied the lateral position at the foot of the bed and of course enjoyed the company of the four pairs of feet which lay lengthways in the conventional manner. At least the night always started out that way and when the lady came to close our door she wafted a sprig of burning lavender about to counteract the flatulence. I was rather more stunned by the feet, I must say!

The fifteen-year-old evacuee had the same Christian name as me – Kenneth – and I suppose his age automatically gave him priority rights, anyway, I was renamed Jimmy almost immediately by the lady, and thenceforth lost my identity for almost nine months.

Mr. and Mrs. Sandford.

I suppose the benefits of throwing open one of your bedrooms to five strange children during the war were few, though I later learned that those who were kind enough and able enough to do so received government payment of ten shillings a week per child. It must have helped! Ration books were your lifeline, and every man, woman and child had one. The coupons, or "Points" as they were called, governed your allowance of meat, eggs, fruit and sweets. You were allowed four rashers of bacon per month, four eggs, two oranges, a quarter pound of sweets, and so on.... Anything desirable that you saw in shops seemed to have the verbal attachment "You can't have them – you haven't got enough points, my love!"

Because of their obvious value to every one, the ration books of all were spirited away to a bureau in the lady's bedroom downstairs for safekeeping and judicious administration. In fact, the rare illuminated manuscripts of a monastic order could not have benefited better from this particular degree of safekeeping, for we were never to set eyes on them or their entitlements again during our stay at Southville Rd. They became however, the key to my memory bank on this particular evacuation episode, because when we all five resolved to run away and get back to Bristol, we knew we just couldn't leave without our ration books.

Months of misery ensued as, along with the other evacuees Ken, Dennis and Peter, we struggled to survive. The school we attended was also less than welcoming as our presence there was regarded as detrimental to the smooth running it had enjoyed prior to the evacuation scheme. We seemed to be at odds with the teachers most of the time, and certainly "ran the gauntlet" with the local bullies on most days. These events, along with unpalatable food served to us at a separate table from the family, simply hardened our resolve.

The youngest and smallest was the obvious choice to negotiate the trail to the bureau in the lady's bedroom without detection. So, in the dead of night I was detailed to exit the bedroom and make my way by the upper landing window, (the stairs were locked off), across the greenhouse roof of glass, to the back garden and thence into the house through the back door – always unlocked because the lavatory was outside. Not for our use, mind you, because we had a po in the bedroom. The task was to enter the lady's bedroom without waking her or Mr Sandford, and to remove the five ration books from her bureau.

As it happened, I came away with seven, but that's another story. Meanwhile the older Ken, my brother John, along with Dennis and Peter, had donned clothes over their pyjamas and crept out of the front door with the suitcases. As a gesture of defiance and at further risk, I re-entered the house and released the budgie from its cage.

We made our way jubilantly to the railway station at 4 am that morning, each of us buoyed by the knowledge that soon we'd be home with Mum.

To get on to the platform at the station it was necessary to cross an overhead bridge which was covered in, and it was when we were midway across this bridge that hearts leapt into mouths as we saw a flashing torch searching the darkness at the other end... As a group we quickly contrived to be a pile of luggage by sitting on the cases and throwing Ken's mac over us, hardly breathing in the hope that he would pass us by. Unfortunately, the deception lasted very briefly for an astute Weston bobby.

We told him we'd run away and had to get a train back to Bristol. He listened sympathetically, and then assured us that we would be allowed

The policeman on Weston-Super-Mare station overhead bridge.

to run away in the morning, but for tonight we had to return to Southville Rd. I for one believed him implicitly.... he was a policeman!

So we were turned in, and were all given a good hiding, taken in turns. Mr and Mrs Sandford were no doubt pleased to recover the ration books, particularly as two of them had their names on the front. I think it goes without saying that as a seven-year-old under some pressure, I didn't bother much about establishing ownership of each one; it was also very dark in the bedroom! A number of lectures on the value of ration books seem to be dotted over the next few weeks.

I did enjoy a sense of individual heroism with the whole affair because my punishment entailed eating on my own in the scullery for some time. Ken, John, Dennis and Peter would pinch extra food from the table and give me treats out of compassion.

Those days I'm sure sowed the seeds in me, as they would have done in many, for a fine crop of truculence and cynicism. Seeing the humour in most of these situations and responding untypically did not serve to endear me to the Sandfords.

Fancy putting me at a table by myself with minimal servings of food and an empty budgie cage! It made me laugh in spite of myself. Only another clout with the stump brought forth the required tears. I think I learnt not to cry because I knew that it was expected. I told myself that all the deprivation and all the hurt was in fact not happening to me and I became an impartial observer:

"Where's that **Jimmy?**"

"**Jimmy**, you come here and get this cleaned up."

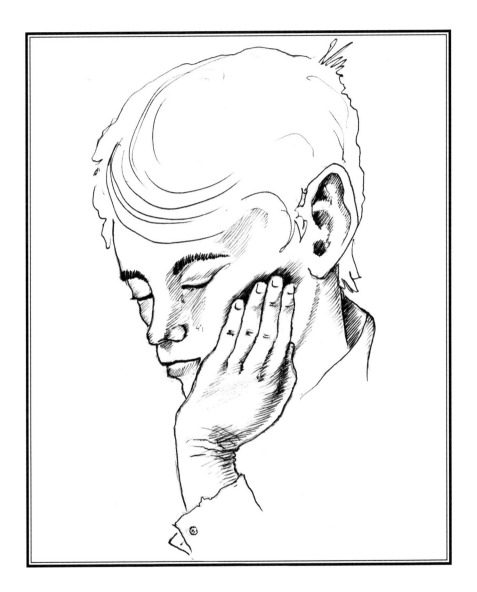

"I learnt not to cry"

"You can all go, but **Jimmy's** to stop home" – You see,

It wasn't me at all – it was that little bugger **Jimmy**.

When John and I planned to leave Weston we were somewhat helped by the stir that was caused when Peter's mother arrived to take him home. The performance that was orchestrated for her was not lost on us.

We all sat in the front room – a room we had never been allowed in. All five evacuees were on the settee. There was tea in matching cups and saucers and a big plate of seed cake. Mrs Sandford had found a different voice from somewhere and used it to glide Peter's mother into an opposite armchair. Throughout their tea-party talk wherein Peter was given a status that he had never enjoyed before, many watery smiles were aimed at us by Mrs Sandford. Her every comment was backed up by a devoted husband who stood beside her seated figure, which had the amusing effect of giving them the same height.

Never, never had there been five more happy and contented children than these "rather fortunate" evacuees. With the help of a good husband – who by the way, was more than willing to serve again – but – see for yourself! The money can't come anywhere near the actual costs of feeding them! But, you do what you can as part of the War Effort! They are absolutely devoted to us, and ... what will we do when it's all over and we have to give them back...

It was at about this point in the "charade" that Dennis farted. This was not so much a comment as a timely punctuation that sent all five of us into paroxysms of stifled laughter. It was also an opportune moment for Mrs Sandford to desperately cover by suggesting..."More tea.. Mrs. er' um?"

Her departure, along with Mr. Sandford who helped her carry the teapot, saw Peter fly across the room into his mother's arms. I suppose it was only then that we realised that she was one of us.

Peter's small case had been packed and on the top was an apple and his sacred ration book.

When the teapot returned and the cake was eaten, an astonishing piece of information was released. It seems that every ration book had to be registered with the local shops and Peter's mother said she had no use for the old book as she flourished a brand new one in Peter's name.

This revelation meant, simply, that we had no need to feel anchored in Weston-Super-Mare, we could just walk, just simply walk, at anytime.

A couple of days later – we did.

John and I went to school as usual, and at the end of the day we set out on the road to Bristol instead of going home to "Stalag Southville." It took ages to get out of the town and onto country roads but when we did it must have been obvious to road users that we were on a greater mission than just going home for tea. Who helped us I can't recall as I think I slept most of the way.

I would like to know what was said by Kenneth and Dennis in order to cover our escape as long as possible. I don't remember their other names and we never saw them again. I was just happy to arrive back in Bristol as Ken and leave Jimmy in Weston.

CHAPTER 5

"Piss freely for four hours." Well, that's what it said on the directions in the packet. Was it possible? The small brown envelopes were to be found everywhere in Bristol during the latter months of 1943. They were a free supply to American servicemen and must have been dropped from a plane like propaganda leaflets, so prolific were they at this time. We collected them from the streets, the docks, the pub pavements (and in bulk from the G.I. dumps). The small brown envelope contained a balloon that was rolled up and a white paper with directions on it, the most memorable of these being, "following intercourse, piss freely for four hours.." I later realised that it simply meant "as often as you can". The yanks had been around for some time and I can recall how much smarter they looked in their top-quality gabardine uniforms than our own British Tommies bedecked in often ill-matched blanket type khaki. Looking back, I suppose injured pride alone was enough to justify the many street scuffles that we witnessed, though when I later learned that the Americans were in Britain for almost two years before going to the front, I'm amazed that the attrition rate wasn't higher than at Guadalcanal. They had it all, it seemed. Smart uniforms, money to spend, gifts galore and interminable leave.

Military badges, shrapnel, and cigarette cards were the currency among Bristol kids and the arrival of the Yanks added French letters and Chiclets as units of exchange. A goodly supply of any of these could ensure you a life on easy street, though if you had a sister things might have been a thousand-fold better. At least that was my seven-year-old presumption, because it was the question most often asked me by the Yanks.

"The Mauretania" was a pub in Bristol that had been built using the salvaged material from a sunken ship of the same name. Its windows were the old portholes, many of which had the nose of yours truly pressed hard against them at night, listening to the strains of songs such as "I'll see you again" or "Somewhere in France with you". My mum was a singer there, and would entertain nightly when she had finished pushing carriages up and down the goods yard alongside Italian P.O.W's. at Temple Meads Station during the day. Those officers whose uniforms were slung carelessly or hurriedly about our sparse apartment in Ashley Rd were probably unaware until they raised an arm in salute, that their tunic had lost a button, a badge or a decoration of some kind. I had a good collection... for a while I think I was the only source of Purple Hearts.

The Yanks traded in silk stockings, candy bars, cigarettes and comics of all kinds which they seemed to procure very cheaply at a place called the P.X. But we soon discovered that every G.I. camp had its own freely dispensing cornucopia of these things which they called the Garbage. A G.I. garbage dump was the most amazing supermarket of tinned and packet goods, comics, chiclets, footwear, socks, containers and comestibles of all kinds... camp beds and steel lockers, cartons of cigarettes, etc, the list is endless. Who was it who coined the phrase "Over supplied Over sexed and Over here", as the three main criticisms of the American forces? There seemed to be some truth in the first part anyway. Since the loss of my shrapnel collection with the bombing of Scapens pub, I'd concentrated on badges and comics, mostly, as these were easily tradeable with other kids. However, the advent of the French letter packets, with instructions, and the ever ready need for cigarettes, opened up a whole new market for me among adults. I set out to accumulate a stock of both.

"Gotnee gum chum?"

Swapping, bartering, wheeling and dealing saw me get through such prizes as a "King Conker", a bag of blood orange marbles, or "Aggies" as we called them then. A piece of a barrage balloon that was burnt around the edges, bundles of Champion comics and even a piece of metal from a downed Messerschmitt. All had passed through the ever outstretched hands of "Our Gang" in exchange for the stock that we each sought.

It was at about this time that my mother married again. Charlie Waters was his name and I remember him as a thin man in a grey suit. The only other memory was the clip over the ear which preceded the confiscation of 500 cigarettes in a large flat Craven 'A' tin, and the Bisto box filled with carefully stacked French letters, 'plus instructions.'

We never saw much of Charlie Waters because it happened at a time when my brother and I were between billets and very soon after his arrival we were evacuated to a place called Devizes. I think it might have been friends or relatives of Charlie Waters that we were sent to in Devizes. It was certainly arranged very quickly and was no doubt convenient to have us placed in a bedroom thirty or so miles away than just next door.

In retrospect, the decision to place this little town in Wiltshire on the list of safe areas for evacuees must have come to the War Office in a direct communiqué from Goering. It was after all the site of the biggest Army base in the U.K. at the time. Small wonder then that we were back at Ashley Road in Bristol within a month having been bombed out of billets twice as we ducked for cover from Jerry's excess load, dropped on his return from missions to Liverpool, Birmingham and Coventry.

There seemed to be lots of Yanks around which wasn't a bad thing given their generous nature towards kids, but John and I were moody, still living off unhappy memories of Weston-Super-Mare. This little town was a most unlikely target in the overall scheme of German aerial bombardment and all seemed pastoral and serene. It was a surprise to everyone to be blasted from their beds by a near miss at the end of our street.

I don't think anyone suffered injury on that occasion but the burst water mains caused such flood havoc that we had to be moved to another house. We must have only been there four or five days.

John and I often referred in later life to the experience of the next foster home. We don't remember her name, but she had two teenage daughters who were sadists! We never had so many baths in all our lives, certainly, we had no more or less aversion to soap and hot water than any other kids of our age, but being dumped in the galvanised tin-bath every night seemed a bit excessive! Worse than that though, was the fact that we were *scrubbed*.

These two daughters from hell took to us with the stiff scrubbing brushes that were normally used on the floors. Every night this ritual took place in spite of tears and pleading. Thank God! relief finally came when another five hundred pound high explosive was off-loaded causing their house of horrors to lean out over the street at an angle of 45 degrees. It made it unusable and it was condemned.

Shame in a way – that's a door I'd liked to have knocked on when I went back at the age of twenty-one.

Being scrubbed at bath time by a teenage sadist!

CHAPTER 6

As a child I associated Cheddar with cheese and not the Gorge which is to be found about twenty miles south of Bristol, and my brother John and I were to be evacuated to a new foster home near Cheddar Gorge.

As we had been bombed out of our last billet in Devizes, we were returned home, for which we were very grateful to the German High Command. Our succession of unsatisfactory billets was beginning to brand us with a reputation for delinquency, and the authorities in Bristol were given to much tongue clicking and heavy sighs when the Beachem boys were mentioned.

I remember the bus journey took about three hours, and the bus was full of mothers and children. We'd been given emergency rations – a tin of corned beef, a tin of condensed milk and a slab of milk chocolate each. These were in the case for about the first ten minutes of the journey before we decided that it was an emergency and we'd have to open the chocolate. All the kids were smeared with it before long.

We stopped at small villages here and there and some people would get off, until finally the bus was left with six evacuees going to Cheddar. When we arrived it was dark and an A.R.P. Warden escorted us into a school or church hall where we were given more sweets and a chance to use the lavatory. Some other evacuees were already there and had come in from other cities.

For some reason not known to us we had to bed down for the night in this hall, and while stretched out on palliasses with our heads on our gas mask cases, the A.R.P. Warden filled us in on some local history. We were somewhere in the Mendip Hills, and he told us of nearby caves called Wookey Hole – in itself a scary name, I thought. He went on to describe how the caves were formed, and that they had names like, "Hell's Passage", "Witch's Parlour", "Witch's Hall and Kitchen" named after a witch who was believed in the Middle Ages to live there and eat the local children. I don't know about John but I certainly didn't sleep that first night.

Breakfast was brought in by the W.V.S.. and we had porridge with real cream, toast with jam and steaming tin mugs of tea. All through the day people were coming and going as evacuees were allotted their billets. Once or twice John and I were called forward and were looked up and down – we felt like we were in a jumble sale. What was happening, it seemed, was that the local villagers who were going to take evacuees came and looked at you, and if they liked the look of you, they took you. They were well paid for this, mind you – they didn't do it out of patriotism. Ten shillings a head per week plus ration books, and at this time the average wage was only about three pounds.

The onset of a second night at this hall saw the arrival of more evacuees, and it began to look less and less likely that we would be chosen. There was also an impending repeat of the previous night's horror stories for the new arrivals to be considered. John pulled out the tail of his vest to polish his multi-lensed glasses and said to me: "Get yer things we're goin' home".

We dropped our case out of the window behind us then asked if we could go to the lavatory. The A.R.P. man said: "You can't go together, the littlun can go first, then when he comes back you can go". I was thunderstruck because we'd intended to go past the lavatory and out

I doubt that John's eyes benefited much from his glasses: he looked sideways to compensate for the cracks in his lenses.

of the next door which exited the hall into a gravelled road. John hissed, "You go on, I'll be out in a minute!"

I was sweating as I stepped out into the cold night and I didn't know which way to go. I thought I'd better go round the back and get our case. The grass was long and wet and it was very dark because of the blackout precautions. I tried to remember the shape of the hall inside and work my way round to the window. As I came nearer to where it should have been there was a loud Bang! I froze rigid there in the long wet grass till John came up to me out of the gloom. "I jumped out the window and landed on our case – it's broke". "C'mon, you gotta help me find my glasses – they came off". He dragged me back to the window where he stuffed the corned beef and condensed milk down my overcoat, found his glasses and hauled me to the edge of the road. "Hurry up" he said, "or they'll catch us... Why're you walkin' like that? Oh God no! You've gone and done it in yer trousers haven't you?" I cried and followed at a stiff-legged distance.

CHAPTER 7

With no knowledge of geography and an even vaguer sense of how far we were from home, we set out along the tree-lined road that led somewhere away from the church or school hall we had left in the Mendip Hills. My brother took the tins of corned beef and condensed milk to his own pockets once he'd seen that I was having difficulty walking. He was nine and I was seven, and we were determined to get back home once again following the third attempt by the authorities in Bristol to evacuate us from home and Mother. We must have spent an hour putting distance between us and the hall. It was cold and dark and it was raining on and off. I was in considerable personal distress and in need of water to clean myself up.

We moved off the road then and into farmland, hoping to find a trough or a haystack. There seemed to be nothing but moors and rocky outcrops as far as we could see. I took to carrying my trousers and had my overcoat safety-pinned between the knees for warmth. A stone crib, built to give the animals some protection in severe weather gave us our first shelter, and I dipped my trousers in the stagnant water of the tin bath it contained. We hammered at the corned beef tins with stones in an effort to get at the meat inside – but all to no avail, and when you're both tired and hungry, one desire always predominates over the other. We fell into deep sleep wrapped together against the cold wind.

The warm sun had almost baked us dry by the time we woke and I was able to wear my trousers again. John went a bit higher up to have a look around and when he came back he drew in the dirt with a stick.

"We're here and down below us is the road. There's a village over to the right and a big town further on," he paused to sniff up then wipe a runny nose on his sleeve. "Over t'other side of this hill there's a farmhouse with a big chicken run". His eyes tilted to mine and we said quietly together..... "Eggs!" No further thought of journeying home could be entertained until we had had something to eat. At this time we were still wearing our transit luggage labels, so we tore these off and buried them under a small pile of stones, along with the condensed milk and corned beef.

Hidden by a copse of trees we came right up to the wire of the chicken run and watched for a while for any sign of human activity. There seemed to be no one about... The hens made a lot of noise when we lifted the latch of the door and entered the run. Moving very quickly, we put about eight eggs in John's rolled jersey front and turned to make a rapid exit with them, when she spoke: "You must be real hungry to be doin' that then" and her rosy face poked out from the hen house. "Where'd you two come from?" John and I couldn't speak for a minute, we never dreamed there'd be anyone inside the hen house.

She was the wife of the farmer, and turned out to be a wonderfully warm and caring lady, not the least bit cross with us as we'd expected her to be. There was no telling off, nor a hiding. In fact she took us inside the farmhouse and gave us breakfast of bacon, eggs and fried bread. In between mouthfuls John told her we'd been evacuated from Bristol to a town up the road and because the lady got sick we were allowed to go home. "What town was that then?" she asked. John spluttered bits of egg, coughed, thought a bit, then scratching his head turned to me saying "What was it Ken, d'you remember?" but my eyes were on my plate as I shook my head vigorously. She seemed to

On the Mendips we hid in stone cribs or haystacks and worked our way towards Bristol.

chuckle a lot at everything we said, and she made a warm bath for us. As we sat facing each other and soaping up, her husband came in and she repeated our story to him. He sucked thoughtfully on a pipe and grunted and nodded. Then he said in his thick Somerset accent, "Well boys, oim pleased you niver run off wi' moi aigs! And when you'm droi, Oi'll tek you in the village n' see the vicar... He'll know wha't'do."

The farm lady gave us sixpence each and helped us up onto the back of the open draycart. As we made our way towards the village, sitting on the back edge, our feet dangling, John enquired, "Where you takin' us then Mister?" "To the village" he said. "Where's that?" asked John. He removed his pipe to use as a pointer..."Down ther! Tha's *Wookey*, an' way over yonder tha's *Wales*!"

Our eyes brightened and there was a quick flash of something shared between us, because we both knew that Wales was quite close to Bristol and therefore we were headed in the right direction. Few road signs were left intact because of the threat of German invasion and local knowledge was the best compass to any destination. Too young by far to appreciate the expression that "a little knowledge is a dangerous thing", our spirits soared at the thought that we were heading for home. However, we had no wish to waste time with the local vicar and perhaps end up back at the church hall.

The broad Somerset farmer continued to talk and point with his pipe until he was out of earshot, and we watched from behind a hawthorn hedge till he rounded the next bend, and then we headed off very fast through a field of turnips.

CHAPTER 8

John and I scuttled across the field of turnips and into a ditch on the far side. In all probability the Somerset farmer was still talking to us and pointing out interesting landmarks with his pipe, not knowing that we had dropped quietly from the back of his cart some five minutes before. We had no wish to be taken to the local vicar for inevitable interrogation and return to the authorities.

The farmer had pointed out Wales to us on the skyline and we knew that Bristol was nearby. Our Aunty May often talked about having her holidays over in Wales. We pressed on over more fields of turnips or beet and, keeping to the ditches when we saw the Land Army girls hoeing, we headed all the time towards Bristol and Wales. Late in the afternoon the thunder of an approaching rainstorm and the blackened sky added to our certainty that we wouldn't be in Bristol that night. But we kept on going, blinded by the homing instinct that drives all sensible reasoning from your mind.

When it became almost too dark to see we came upon a road that led us toward a cliff face. and a stone pillar that had a metal plate on it. This announced that we were at the entrance to *Wookey Hole*. Although the torrential rain had begun, we both found renewed energy and a carefree disregard for the wet discomfort of staying on the road that would bypass the dry caves. Our friendly A.R.P. man had told us all we needed to know of *"Hell's Passage"* and the *"Witch's Kitchen"* and the story of the witch who ate children lent wings to our heels. We spent the rest of the night in a damp haystack, fitfully dozing and waiting for the daylight to reappear. In the morning we got a lot further on our way when a Land Army Girl potted us and gave us a ride on her tractor. She shared her sandwiches and cake with us too, and because she was pulling a trailer of turnips and apples, we soon became very full and so were our pockets.

When she had to turn off the road, John and I decided it was the best way to travel and we'd only have to wait for another vehicle to come along and we'd be home before teatime.

We didn't have long to wait! As the little black car eased to a stop beside us, our hearts skipped a beat or two because the driver wore the reversed collar of a clergyman. It must be the vicar that our Somerset farmer had been taking us to. Rather reluctantly we climbed into the back seat of his car as he asked our names and where we were going. "Are you the vicar?" asked John. "No, I'm not" he said, laughing. "I was at one time, but now I'm the Dean at Wells Cathedral". We weren't sure what that meant, but decided he was O.K. because he gave us a small bar of Frys Cream chocolate.

We'd never been in a car before and John asked why he had a swastika on the gear stick. He patiently dealt with all the questions before asking again where we were heading for. "We're goin' home to Bristol" I said. "You're a long way from there boys, and you're going in the wrong direction", he said. "No" said John emphatically, "Bristol's near to Wales and Wales is up ahead". "I'm afraid you've been misinformed boys – up ahead is *Wells*, I know because I've lived there for many years". Our hearts hit the pits of our stomachs at this news and we sank into a disappointed silence until the Dean drove through some large gates and up to his house. We thought he must be pretty rich to live in a place this big, and he had servants as well; and a cook.

The Dean of Wells – "Would you like to meet some other Bristol boys"

We had rice pudding in the kitchen and some bread and jam while the Dean busied himself elsewhere in the house. The cook was a bit like our Gran and when we'd eaten she showed us the parlour and the library... I'd never seen so many books.

When the Dean reappeared he asked if we'd like to meet some other Bristol boys! "Yeah, all right" we said, not knowing how he was going to manage that. He then took us in his car to a house a few streets away, and John and I couldn't believe our eyes. Here in the town of Wells were two of our friends from Newfoundland Rd School, Tony and Gordon Leach. They'd been evacuated here about a month ago and were living with this elderly couple who ran a drapery shop in the main road. What a time we had that night, John and I in one bed and Tony and Gordon in the other talking till late about home and the bombing, our escape from Weston-Super-Mare and our more recent experiences in the Mendip Hills and Wookey Hole. They were pretty homesick too but they were comfortable and well looked after here, and they even liked the school they were at in Wells. Tony and Gordon were brothers aged ten and eight respectively and they lived in Byron Street quite close to our old school. We didn't play much together because we were in different classes but we knew them well.

Before going to sleep we told them of our resolve to get back home again come what may. We knew the Dean had prevailed on the old couple to take us in and see how we turned out, but we had no intention of staying on longer than this one night. When the next day dawned we put our plans into operation.

CHAPTER 9

It had been a big surprise to John and I to find two other evacuees from our school living with an elderly couple in Wells. After spending a warm night there, and fortified with breakfast we set off with Tony and Gordon Leach for the local school. We had no intention of completing that journey mind you, but we had to agree because the Dean of the Cathedral had made the arrangements. It was he who'd given us a lift into Wells the day before. However, we weren't completely without honour as we decided to leave the sixpence each that we had on the bedroom sideboard.

Tony had shown us his school atlas, which provided us with a better idea of the way to go in our intention to get home to Bristol. Up to now we'd been travelling blind from Cheddar way and had headed for what we were told was "Wales". Signs were sparse because of the expected German invasion, but because Wells was quite small we soon found ourselves in open country again. Tony had given us his school lunch as he could easily get another he said, and as we left, he and his brother Gordon called out "Don't go an' shit yerself again." I gave John a hard punch on the arm for telling him.

We now had to face the Mendip Hills once again and follow the road to Chewton Mendip. After that we would have about another twelve miles to get to Bristol. We climbed and puffed for most of that morning and carried our coats for a good part of it because it was so warm. We were no longer encumbered with our suitcase and gas masks as these had been left behind several nights ago when we ran away from the church hall. We ate Tony's sandwiches on a bluff over-

*looking the main road. We had to keep the road in sight at all times but our lesson had been learnt to avoid being seen or assisted by well meaning people. As a result, we had many diversions around thick bramble and streams, which resulted in scratched bleeding legs and wet shoes and socks.

When we took a rest in the afternoon on a higher piece of ground, we could see up ahead a lot of activity. They were coal mines, and there were workers coming and going everywhere, so it looked as if we had no choice but to take to the road. We decided to try and have a sleep then and see how far we could get by walking the straight road during the dark hours of night. It wasn't really possible to sleep in the bright light of the afternoon, but we were certainly very tired and the few hours till dark became noticeably colder. By the time we moved onto the road, a thick fog was coming down over the countryside and hand in hand we moved gratefully in what was now a straight line towards home.

The fog was damp and eerie and John and I took to singing as we padded along the side of the road. We'd learnt a lot of songs from listening to Mum at home and when we joined her at the Ice Rink. People said she looked and sang like Dorothy McGuire the filmstar. It passed the time and gave us a rhythm for walking, and it also helped to give us a feeling that we were not alone out there.

It was very late and I suppose we were unguarded by tiredness when a vehicle picked us up from behind with its headlights. We were in a cutting at the time and there was just no escape. There we stood like two blinded hedgehogs caught in a narrow band of light. "Hey kids, how ya doin'? Kinda late gettin' home from school huh?" It was an American Army jeep preceding a convoy of trucks. A soldier in a peaked cap came towards us with a cheery grin and we were soon hoisted into the back of one of the trucks with a crowd of friendly Yanks. They plied us with chewing gum, chocolate, and a multitude of questions. They were based somewhere between Chewton Mendip and Bristol and were returning from night manoeuvres. We roared on through the dark toward home, denying that we were German spies or parachutists.

When we pulled up inside the camp, the officer detailed one soldier to see that we got supper and a bed, and two grateful evacuees slept till late the next morning knowing that Chewton Mendip was well behind us. We were also secure in the knowledge that a supply truck was going to take us as far as Knowle on the outskirts of Bristol. We knew our way from there day or night.

We were piled up with American comics, Hershey bars and Chiclets when we left finally on the supply truck and the next few miles saw numerous stops at which we helped the G.I. Corporal to load and unload goods. As it had been late in the morning when we woke the best part of the day had long gone and it was twilight over Bristol when we jumped down in the main road through the suburb of Knowle. John and I smiled when we saw the sign – it was Wells Road.

We made our way quickly down to Temple Meads Station where Mum worked during the day but didn't stop because during the week she always sang at the Mauretania Pub in the city.

At about 9 p.m. that night, just five days after leaving, two dishevelled but proud faces had noses pressed to the porthole windows of The Mauretania while Mum sang in an amber glow to the assembled armed forces.

The W.V.S. woman.

CHAPTER 10

It seemed to rain for weeks after we came home from Cheddar, and although Mum was cross with us for turning up again and making trouble for her with the authorities, we were all very happy to be together again. Several times we were visited by the W.V.S., and we had an idea that before long we'd be sent out of Bristol on another attempt to billet us away from the persistent bombing raids.

Our Anderson shelter was waterlogged by now, and whenever the sirens went at night John and I, Mum, and Aunty May would crouch in a cupboard under the stairs holding on to the gold cross that Mum wore around her neck until the all clear went. My Gran slept on upstairs merely grunting vexedly as Aunty May left the bed. I remember the simple prayers that John and I squeezed through tears, holding on to Mum's gold cross necklace. "Please God, don't let the planes come over tonight! but if they do, don't let them drop bombs on Bristol, but if they do, don't let them hit our place... but if they do, don't let us be killed." It was a prayer you could start when the siren went, and add to as the course of the war changed above your head.

It's uncanny to realise what skills were developed in the face of abject terror at this time. It's a fact that all the kids I knew then were able to tell what sort of aircraft was approaching by the sound of its engines. The siren would wail in that urgent undulating tone that turned your bowels to water, and as all the lights went out and the searchlights came on, a tense stillness came over everything. You strained to pick up the first drone of engines. "It's all right they're ours," someone would say, and we'd breathe again. But if the continuous note of the

All Clear didn't sound we knew we could expect more. Often a small group, or even a single aircraft would pass over in the black night and it was easier to isolate whether we were under threat from Dorniers, Focke Wolfs, Junkers 88's or Messerschmitt fighters.

This specialised knowledge was reinforced by posters and charts that seemed to be everywhere, which showed the black silhouette of enemy aircraft from the side and underneath view. I was a bit surprised when I later saw at close quarters a Focke Wolf aircraft that had been shot down over Durdham Down, a rather sleek brown machine that wasn't black at all. Nights of particularly heavy raids would have the Bristol skies throbbing, as squadron after squadron of German bombers made their way up the Severn River on course for the industrial areas of the Midlands. "Birmingham's gonna get it tonight," we'd be saying. At the same time we knew they'd be coming back the same way, always with a bit left over for the docks and Avonmouth. There'd be fears, tears and trepidation all through the night until they'd passed over again.

School carried on as usual now, but earlier in the war the schools closed because everyone was supposed to be evacuated to the country or smaller towns. This resulted in hundreds of kids roaming the streets, and parents who held firm to the resolve that they weren't going to send their children away were threatened with prosecution. The weight of numbers compelled the Government to open city schools again and keep going as best they could with a floating roll.

Not surprisingly the children had some definite opinions on the situation which varied according to their personal priorities. Ten-year-olds would say "War's a damned nuisance, everything's on coupons, you can't even get sweets!" While thirteen-year-olds believed that – "There never ought to be wars, if we were governed properly. There's

Shopkeeper – "You can't 'ave them... you 'amt got 'nuff points."

always old people in power and young people grow up restless. I've been to so many schools since the war's been on I can't settle down."

Pursuit of an education was a crusade for some people while others picked up what they could when the conditions suited them. I suppose John and I fell into the latter category, though we weren't delinquent. Our crusade in life was to stay where Mum, Gran, and Aunty May were and see it through.

Long hours in the Anderson shelter, a lack of water for washing, general shortages of good food and clothing made you not only grubby but also listless and debilitated. In fact, too tired to be naughty! Well, for the most part.

I remember Mum was very proud of her nylon stockings, when she could get them, which wasn't very often. In between times she painted her legs with a tanning cosmetic. Nylons, of course, had a seam down the back. So in order to complete the illusion, a seam had to be drawn in carefully down the line of the calf and ankle with an eyebrow pencil, or sometimes a burnt matchstick. This was a precision job usually delegated to Aunty May, but on the times she wasn't available John or I did it for her. Not always successfully, I might add, but then I can't remember ever seeing a lady with perfectly straight seams on her stockings in those days.

When her birthday was due that September, John and I decided to get Mum some nylons. The best source of supply was the Yankee soldiers of course though why that should be I don't know. Perhaps they were trained to strangle the Germans and not shoot them! You also seemed to have a better chance of trading with them if you had a sister to offer it seemed. However, with the resourcefulness peculiar to kids with a mission, and armed with the knowledge we had of G.I. requirements back on the road from Cheddar we began a very active campaign of swapping and collecting the very best quality comics that we could find. They had to be clean, not torn and of the type that typified adventure and/or mystery. Comics like the Wizard or the Champion, for example.

While accumulating the stock we spent some time testing the market by quizzing the G.I's. who frequented 'Scapens' our local pub on the corner of Monk St. We would show samples of the comics and make the offer of another dozen just as good in exchange for a pair of nylon stockings, but as the 18th of September drew ever nearer our hopes diminished. We had long reached our target of twenty-five good comics without arousing a great deal of interest from our chosen market. I think we had all but given up on the idea and were entertaining the sale of the comics to buy some smelly soap when John made a breakthrough.

It must have been about the 15th and John rushed in breathlessly from the street. He said he'd just come past Scapens and a Yank we'd talked to a few days before asked him if we still had the comics. He said he'd bring the nylons the next evening and we had to meet him outside Scapens with the comics at 7 o'clock. I've never known twenty four hours go so slowly. The Yank was as good as his word and better – the formal exchange of parcels took place at the appointed time next evening. When the morning of Mum's birthday arrived we all sat on the bed to enjoy her open-mouthed surprise at her present of four pairs of nylons.

That Yank must have been a fast reader though because he left the comics with Mr Scapen to return to us, and as a result we were able to swap them again as we worked towards Fireworks Day that was coming up pretty soon.

CHAPTER 11

The priority for evacuation in Britain's wartime fell into very simple categories. They were "A" top priority – schoolchildren aged five to fifteen; "B" children under five; and categories "C" and "D" covered the blind, and expectant mothers. I think I'd have given anything then to be blind or an expectant mother.

The authorities misguidedly thought I was safer away from Bristol and umpteen miles away from home and my mother. At the age of seven and eight I had very few priorities, but home and Mum certainly came at the top of the list. Part of Jerry's conspiracy of course was to persuade England that the bombs dropped outside of Bristol were less lethal. I was able to tell them otherwise after being bombed out of three evacuation billets in the space of eight months. But having the roof blown off, or being the only house left standing intact in an entire street didn't begin to approach the dangers inherent in trying to get back home once the miseries of separation took hold, along with the awareness that the points left in your ration book often dictated your worth and your popularity as an evacuee. The one saving grace for me during these years was that I was always billeted with my brother John.

Following our successful escape from Weston-Super-Mare and Cheddar, and being bombed out of Devizes, the faceless people behind the evacuation scheme decided on somewhere more distant, less appealing, harder for an eight-year-old to find on the map and certainly harder to escape from. They called it Exeter; to me it was Colditz. The train journey was forever, and all the countryside between distorted with tears. We arrived in the dark too, which added to the difficulties because it was important to know where everything was when you were planning to leave again very shortly.

On this occasion, John and I were the only evacuees in the house, and this was certainly better than at Weston where there were five of us all in the same bed. The lady seemed all right and the food was good and I began to think this might turn out all right after all, maybe John and I could take our time formulating the escape plan, instead of rushing it and making mistakes as we did during our first attempt at Weston. We had separate beds this time and that was something totally new to us – certainly it introduced me to the experience of sleeping right through the night. Up until then we had always been put into the same bed, and my brother had been an inveterate bed-wetter since contracting Scarlet Fever when he was much younger. We were given dressing gowns as presents, and were allowed a small part of the garden in which to grow our own flowers. It's interesting in retrospect how the percentage of bed-wetters escalated with the knowledge that enuretics were worth an extra two shillings!

I didn't like the school there much, but on the whole this began to look as if it just might be bearable. The lady held your hand going down the street and took your cap off for you if you met someone – I felt quite posh!

Street activities were different from home because there weren't the bomb sites to play on, but I remember playing "War Games" with other kids at this time. Sides were picked by nominated team leaders, who then approached each other heel and toe, the last complete foot winning first choice. The sides were always Rommel's men and Monty's Eighth Army, and, set out on some suitable open space we

War games on the bomb sites.

would join battle vigorously in what was called Desert Warfare. In simple terms this meant throwing handfuls of sand pinched from the sandbags to see who would be blinded enough to retreat – it was very effective; and even those who played Rommel's men knew the wisdom of allowing Monty to win. Perhaps if these tactics had been known in North Africa, it might have shortened the war!

All in all, Exeter was measuring up pretty well and the first four weeks went by without the time or need to try and arrange an escape back to Bristol. And then the bomb dropped! The lady had a Morrison Shelter in the living room which also served as the dining table, and which gave reasonable safety from falling timber and masonry. Certainly you wouldn't survive a direct hit. On the night of the raid we were ushered from bed to the Morrison with blankets, and everything seemed to follow the usual pattern. First the quiet following the siren, then the approaching drone of heavy bomber aircraft, the first crackle of anti-aircraft fire, followed by the crump of the first bombs. You almost burst from your skin with the tension, and your teeth hurt as you gritted them so hard. Usually it was over in about fifteen minutes, and when this time had elapsed and the sound of heavy engines was fading away, we uncurled and started to talk again. Isn't it funny to think how we all seek safety by wrapping arms around the head? Then, the world erupted! I can't describe the volume of noise that filled the house, as a lone aircraft following the main bunch dropped his stick of high explosives.

How many houses in the street suffered direct hits and how many were reduced to rubble heaps by blast, I don't know, but the fact was that when daylight dawned there was only one house in the entire street left standing and without a roof on it. Jerry had made sure that it would be useless as a haven for two Bristol evacuees. So, after a couple of nights bedded down at the school, we were back on the train and going home.

It must have been almost Christmas in 1943. We chuffed our way into Temple Meads Station, past all the hoarding signs which said all the familiar things like "Ah, Bisto!" or "Support the War Effort", "Buy Bonds", "Is Your Journey Really Necessary." We, as evacuees, felt we had the right answer to that one. "Your Country Needs You" was everywhere, and the bold print poster that said "Don't Talk" was contradicted by the one that said "Tell your A.R.P. Warden, he knows what to do!"

The two nights bedded down in strange blankets at the school in Exeter then gave us two weeks more off in Bristol because we'd both caught the highly contagious skin disease known as scabies. The terrible itch and the ever weeping sores were only soothed by regular visits to the clinic at the Royal Infirmary where we were bathed and smothered in a blue jelly-like soap. It was about this time too that a mass-inoculation programme took place, and you were allowed to wear a red arm band to warn people not to hit you on your sore arm. It didn't work with most kids our age, as it's not only bulls that respond to a red rag!

The snow was heavy that Christmas, and a fashionable mode of dress comprised two pairs of socks on your hands, a scarf covering your head and ears, knotted under your chin, crossed over on your chest and tied at the back. All this over the top of your overcoat. If you could afford some hot chestnuts from the street seller you could warm your pockets with them for a while. There was not much you could do about your feet, they were always wet, it seemed.

Christmas was memorable for the carol singing and the knocking on doors, and the warmth and love of people who cared. In those days everybody seemed to care a great deal more than they did when the war ended. I remember too the stocking which always had an orange pushed into the foot with two new, bright copper pennies.

I don't think we were able to eat anything that was particularly Christmas fare that year, but I've got very happy memories of the foods that we enjoyed then, most of which I've never seen since. My mother would make bread pudding in a meat tray, a moist heavy stodge with a crispy top that you cut into slices, and nothing at all to do with bread and butter pudding as some would insist. There were chitlings and there were faggots, the former being of pig intestine and the latter rather like a small haggis. So Christmas was filled with good food, occasional dry warmth, plenty of copies of the Beano and the Dandy, each of which were sold with a liquorice walking stick or sherbet dab in the centre pages, and there were copies too of the Lion, Hotspur, Chips Own and the irresistible Champion.

Jerry seemed to have taken a holiday, and so too had the evacuation authorities. We dared not think about it, let alone discuss it, just in case we jogged someone's memory. Mind you, we hadn't had too bad a time at the last place. When the dreaded moment came, it was quite unexpected as we were well into January 1944 and had really begun to feel that we were home for good. Our Mum, dressed in her railway uniform and the headscarf that was typical of the time, took us to the pictures at the Metropole as a special treat, because when we got back home she sat us down at the scullery table and said: "I'm sorry my loves, but they've found another home for you in Exeter."

CHAPTER 12

Barely four weeks after being bombed out in Exeter and sent back home to Bristol, my brother John and I were back on the train heading for Exeter once again. Another billet had been found, and this time we weren't quite so miserable because the last one had worked out all right for the most part. I'm sure we'd have spent the rest of the war there if Jerry hadn't taken the roof off the house and flattened all other buildings in the street. But, it's an ill wind... We got to spend Christmas back home in Bristol. Our destination this time was the home of a middle-aged couple who never had any children of their own. They lived at the edge of a heavily wooded area on the outskirts of the city. I mention the woods because they played a large part in our lives at the time and they camouflaged a balloon barrage base staffed by a few men and a substantial number of WAAFs. These balloons were enormous gas-filled silver grey monsters that ascended a few hundred feet up and were tethered to the ground with thick wire cables. They had large ears too, and looked rather like floating elephants up there. The purpose of them was to prevent low-flying aircraft from making successful bombing runs and, of course, from planes landing. They were, no doubt, the origin of the expression "The balloon's gone up" just prior to some action taking place.

The first few days at our new billet were fairly uneventful as John and I got to know the foster parents and they got to know us. The best memory I have of them is that they looked like brothers, too. Mrs Dawson had very short hair, which was unusual for a woman in the 1940's. Mr Dawson always wore a waistcoat over a collarless shirt and he displayed a number of pencils in his top pocket. Apart from some variation in their clothing they therefore were one and the same person to me.

The introductory period over, we were assigned our duties. Blacking the stove once a week was a task to which we brought considerable experience, but scrubbing floors and whitewashing the scullery was something new, and, I might say, that hoeing in the garden wasn't half as pleasurable as it had been when we were allowed to grow our own flowers at the previous billet.

The daily household jobs to be completed before going to school, and then between after school and bedtime, was rewarded with a compulsory tablespoon of castor oil because it was good for you! All of this was compounded by the weekend collection of firewood which seemed to involve everyone in Exeter, and the requirement to attend church, morning, afternoon and evening on Sunday. It took very little more than a furtive glance between John and myself to confirm that an escape plan had to be embarked upon as soon as possible.

Now, I really did eat almost anything as a kid. Wartime was no time to be fussy, after all, but I found that my stomach revolted over boiled potatoes for one, and the margarine that tasted like liquid rubber. It was very hard to avoid the margarine as slices of bread were always pre-spread. But with juvenile cunning, latent acting ability and sleight of hand, the boiled potatoes found their way into my trouser pockets. I escaped detection for some time, but ignorance of the starching qualities of potatoes was to be my undoing! One weekend when the washing was being done, I was questioned by Mrs Dawson on the stiffness of my trouser pockets! Naturally I made a clean breast of it there and then. I told her of my inability to stomach boiled potatoes, and how I spirited them from my plate to the lavatory by means of my pockets. Perhaps a moment's pause preceded the biggest hiding I can ever remember getting, and from then on, *my* truth was always tempered with a bit of judicious cunning, not to mention downright lies!

Many subsequent meals found me at a separate table on my own with bread, cheese and margarine. I would suffer the bread and marg as I pushed the square of cheese to one corner of the slice, knowing that the final two mouthfuls with the cheese added would make the whole thing bearable and hold my stomach down.

Excursions to the woods with a handcart for the purpose of firewood collection was a regular Saturday feature, and gave John and I the chance of meeting up again with Mary, the W.A.A.F. from the balloon barrage base whose generous helpings of bacon and eggs and fried bread through the cookhouse window placed her among the immortals like Monty, Churchill, Gran, and my Mother.

The final straw was when I caught the mumps. These are painful enough, and the swelling made you look like a mating bullfrog; but on top of all that I was sent off to school wearing a *pixie hood*. For God's sake! Didn't Mrs Dawson know I was a boy? The humiliation was indescribable, the laughter and the scorn simply destroyed me and I vowed to quit Exeter as soon as possible.

John was now nearly eleven and was allowed to have a paper round. Although he earned more, he was permitted to keep only sixpence. Mr and Mrs Dawson had applied new rules that meant we were not allowed indoors until five o'clock when Mr Dawson got home and we were eating separately in the scullery. John and I were both blessed with good boy soprano voices, and shortly after arriving at the

Dawsons we were taken on as members of the choir at St. Mary's Church by the steps. We were, after all, spending most of each Sunday in the church with the Dawsons anyway – I've never met anyone since with a greater desire for an after-life.

Each Sunday, two angelic junior members of the choir in red cassocks and white surplices took up the collection down the aisles of St. Mary's and smiled at each member of the congregation as they made their tribute. John and I had decided that the best way to get home was to take the normal route and method that anybody else would if they didn't want to arouse suspicion. We'd had the experience of running away in Weston-Super-Mare and not being well enough pre-pared to avoid questions and ultimate recapture. So, this time we planned a very casual bus trip back to Bristol. It was to be on the normal bus service that did the long distance trips – Green Line it was called – and it would cost eight shillings each to get to Bristol. With John's first sixpence we buried a cocoa tin under a hawthorn bush that Saturday when we went to get firewood.

Every possible effort and endeavour was brought to the fore in our attempt to raise one pound. We needed sixteen shillings for the fare and we reckoned on four more shillings for food and special circum-stances. The comics we had went very quickly at a ha'penny each and John sold a rocket left over from Guy Fawkes day for threepence. We soon realised that our resources were few and the target a long way off. The bitter struggle with potatoes, margarine and castor oil went on relentlessly.

We told Mary of our intentions and she gave us a whole florin which boosted our morale quite a bit. Yet after about a month of effort we seemed to be at a watershed in our savings programme. John felt that

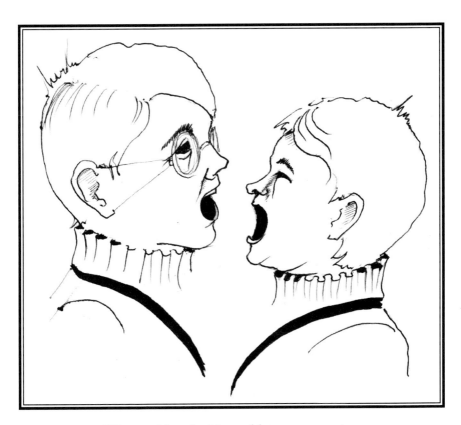

We were blessed with good boy soprano voices.

giving sixpence to the fund left him with absolutely nothing and there was the added problem of having to account to Mrs Dawson for every penny spent.

Drastic actions were then discussed, usually under the bedclothes at night and in whispered tones for fear of being overheard, perhaps not so much by Mr and Mrs Dawson, but by a higher authority.

If we were caught putting this new plan into action the shame and the disgrace would be considerable. But, I thought, would it be any more humiliating than having to wear a Pixie hood to school? How will God feel about it I wondered – but then, what about "God loves little children" and what about "God helps them that help themselves." Gran had often said that. It was all the justification we needed.

During the course of the morning, afternoon and evening services on the following Sunday, with trembling but quite experienced sleight of hand, we spirited the balance of twelve shillings and sixpence from the collection plates, all the while with heads seemingly bowed in reverence, though in fact, in mortal dread of being struck down by lightning at any minute.

Supposedly off to school the next morning, we boarded the bus for Bristol unseen, and arrived at home with the four shillings that we hadn't the stomach to spend en route. I add as a footnote that twenty years later I visited Exeter and made a point of going into "St Mary's by the Steps." I had then the opportunity to say "Thanks for the loan" and to make a contribution to the Church Restoration fund. I also went to the Dawsons but couldn't bring myself to knock.

CHAPTER 13

Having arrived back in Bristol unofficially from Exeter, it wasn't surprising to find that there weren't too many kids to play with, and school at Newfoundland Rd was only part time. Those that were attending were older than John and I, and so we found ourselves with plenty of time on our hands. I expect we were far from being ideal pupils even under the best conditions, but we did seem to score more than our share of what was known as "A Whack 'o' the Dap." This was a punishment rendered more painful by the humiliation suffered than the pain inflicted. The "dap" was the sole of a shoe – plimsolls as they were commonly called – though in Bristol they were always known as daps. At Newfoundland Rd it was kept on view in a glass case high on a wall. Its ceremonial lowering was always met with much cringing by everyone, and the miscreant would be made to bend over at the front of the class. Very few of us had much seat to the trousers anyway and I don't think underpants had been invented then, so I can't say it didn't hurt a bit. But being bent over and whacked on the bum in front of the class...! This was the hardest thing to take, and of course, holding back the tears. Miss Fisk, the headmistress must have had a quota of whackings that she had to give in any one week and when the school roll was depleted by absent evacuees, it meant there was more to be shared between a few of us.

A favourite classroom game during her many temporary absences was a kind of medieval slingshot attack on the far row of kids. It meant pairing up, because you had to use the braces of the next boy to fire your ruler through the air. The ruler would be balanced on your companion's shoulder and pinched back with the elastic braces, and you would instruct up or down, left or right to adjust your aim before releasing the lethal twelve inches. Given the time, you could paint the end of the missile with the blue/black ink from your inkwell. Dart attacks were popular too, and easily made by breaking the points off an old pen nib, leaving two short sharp spears at the side. Flights made of paper were decorated with swastikas, and slid into a split at the back of the nib. They flew more elegantly than the ruler and were certainly not as painful. And so it happened that while joined in battle I was spotted by Miss Fisk through the window of the adjoining corridor, and, following her Spanish Inquisition bit, I was ordered to fetch the long window pole with which she lifted down the dreaded "dap."

I made for the pole standing beside the door, and at the very last second my legs took over control of my mind and body and at the greatest speed I could muster I was gone from the classroom, the school, the dreaded "dap" and had placed the length of Newfoundland Rd between myself and Miss Fisk. The deed was done before I could think about the implications of it. Every second away made it harder to go back so I just kept going all the way home. Mum was at work, I knew that, so I went round to our Gran's place in Monk St. "What bist thee doin' yer?" she asked. "Ive bi bad Gran and I don't wanna go back to school" I said. "Gawd bleed'n 'imey what you bin doin now?"

I told her all about Miss Fisk giving me a whack 'o' the dap all the time and that our John had it plenty of times and it was all over some games we played and we weren't the only one doing it but we always got caught – and before I could finish, she was pushing the hat pin through her black hat and pulling me out the front door by the ear. She clipped me down Newfoundland Rd. to the school and into the classroom, stopping Miss Fisk in full flight and asked to see her out in the corridor. What took place between them I shall never know, but I was moved to the front where I could be watched through narrowed eyes, and I was the last to be let go at the end of the day for weeks. I avoided the "dap" on that occasion and when I got the chance I said "Thanks Gran." She grunted something about tykes bein the death of her and then said, "Don't you dare bring no more trouble home, think I ent got enough to do? And thers a war on! I told that Miss Fisk to deal with you ther' not send you 'ome. You'll get morena dap you come 'ome agen!" I don't really think she meant it though.

CHAPTER 14

After the Exeter episode, I rather think that the evacuation authorities quietly dropped the Beachem file behind a dusty desk in the hope that it wouldn't be found again before the war ended. Some of the four million evacuees that were shunted around England and overseas had been settled quickly and gave no cause for concern throughout the war, but my brother and I seemed to have created a small mountain of paper work and travelled as many footsore miles as an average infantry unit.

We were really a part of an unconscious wave of rebellion against change to the family unit, and to our socio-economic birthright. Being bombed and resettled were categories for which there was some provision in the evacuation scheme, but voluntarily leaving your billet, pinching your own ration books and travelling miles overland to get home again was a rather small file to which my brother and I seemed to make a large contribution. It seemed better to accept our determination, and lose the file, so it looked like being home for good.

I recently came across a statement made by Richard Titmuss, a noted Social Historian, who wrote: "To be torn up from the roots of home life and to be sent away from the family circle, in most instances for the first time in a child's life, was a painful event. The whole of the child's life, its hopes and fears, its dependence for affection and social development on the checks and balances of home life, and all the deep emotional ties that bound it to its parents, were suddenly disrupted. From the first day of September 1939, evacuation ceased to be a problem of administrative planning. It became instead a multitude of problems in human relationships."

Yet I think it's true to say that we as kids were bearing up better than most adults to the privations of war. This is surely because kids are so inventive and willing to accept new conditions and of course to change them if necessary. I think of the war games we played on the very sites of real tragedy, and death. The cardboard tanks we built, the sticky bombs we made which put them out of action. The knowledge of the rule that if the siren went while you were on the way to school, you were to turn around again and go home immediately – if already at school, you were to stay. It was this knowledge that governed the pace at which you walked to school, the object being to give Jerry every possible opportunity to launch a raid before you got there. The congestion at the gates was caused by the desperate hopes of those who wouldn't enter until the last possible minute, and all chance was gone of the wailing siren that would send them careering home again.

Raids which occurred while you were at school brought into action the often-rehearsed procedures for getting to the nearest air-raid shelters. Large numbers of children were actually moved very quickly through the streets by what was known as the "Wave Method." This involved columns of three or four assembling on the pavement to march in a given direction on command, and when the road had to be crossed we were all brought to a halt and with a series of whistle blasts turned to face the opposite pavement, and then moved as one body in a surge across the road. Groups of several hundred were moved very quickly in this way.

The public shelters in Bristol City centre were of dubious solidity, built of red brick and designed not unlike today's public toilets. Most of them seemed to serve both purposes. They had an entrance at each end and a central dividing wall. The drainage and ventilation gap in the corner of this wall was just big enough to squeeze through if you felt inclined to play the time-honoured game of "confuse the teacher" when the counting began.

Many of these shelter areas were severely damaged during bombing, and on reflection it was probably because they looked so much like military installations from the air. It was the result of a crush into one of these shelters on a school day that my brother lost his glasses. John had been a wearer of glasses since he was about four years old and as any dependent knows, they can cause no end of trouble in requiring the care and attention that a child is not used to giving. His glasses were supplied by the Corporation – as we knew it – it was the Health Department I suppose. They were the typical wire frame type of the period. I have seen them worn with one arm only for a long time, and I was familiar with the sight of them in plasters and splints. I doubt that his eyes benefited much from the appearance of bi-focalism that the crack gave to the lens of his left eye. So the humour had certainly gone out of their appearance by the time a high jostling elbow removed them from his nose and dispensed with the one remaining arm. My lasting memory of his glasses is that he wore them for almost another complete year with two loops of string over his ears to hold them on.

It was in the times of being confined to shelters that the songs were sung and the charades performed and the traditions of British Music Hall flourished yet again. And while the adults discovered hidden talents with which they could ease the stress, the kids gave birth to parodies, chants and graffiti the like of which still stays with me. The often-heard Colonel Bogey March was given the lyric:

"Hitler, has only got one ball
Goering, has two but very small
Himmler, has something similar
But poor ol Goebbels has no balls at all."

Whether or not there was any truth in it didn't really matter, it gave us all a laugh at the time.

"Whistle while you work
Hitler is a twerp!
Goering's barmy, so's his army
Whistle while you work."

Then there was the evacuees' anthem sung to the tune of "Old Soldiers Never Die":

"I know a rotten place, far far away called... (whatever)
Where we have bread and jam three times a day.
Egg and bacon never see, never brings us in our tea -
We are gradually fading away."

We all joined in with "We're going to hang out the washing on the Siegfried Line" and of course "Run Rabbit Run" which we've all since heard as the theme tune of the popular T.V. series "Dads Army."

We played desert warfare on the bomb sites and convoy in the gutters, and later in the war we invented "Concentration Camp" although the true horror of these atrocities against humanity was not known until they were overrun. For us as children they were known to be the prisons such as "Stalag Luft 3," where our soldiers and airmen were imprisoned. (The term "concentration camp" was in use well before the discovery of places like Auschwitz and Dachau.) This game involved a team on either side of a fence or railing area, and the object of the game was to overthrow the German guards in order to free the weak prisoners. One such location with ideal iron railings was St Mary Redcliffe church, and the small scar on the inside of my left knee is even today a reminder of being caught up in the spikes of those railings as we were chased out by the vicar. I put a jumping jack in his letter box the following Guy Fawkes for that.

By late 1944 the war seemed to be losing its impetus. There were certainly fewer raids now, and the blackout precautions had been lifted. Mum didn't have to work at Temple Meads Station any more and had a job as a "clippie" on the buses. The uniform was much The same, and so were the hours, it seemed – because she still sang in the Mauretania pub at night. We had a new Uncle too. He was a G.I. who worked at the Disney Studios as an artist before the war. Corporal Gerald Jennings was short, slight and balding and anxious to take us all to America, and he married my mother to prove that he meant it. The implications of how and why he returned with his unit to the United States without my mother is a mystery to me to this day. However, he did turn up again later in life, and we all lived together in Hawarden just outside Christchurch in New Zealand for a full year before he decided to return permanently to America.

The cinemas were beginning to show encouraging news items following that well-known opening theme, and the voice that said "This is the Gaumont British News, The Eyes And Ears Of The World." Cheers would go up in the cinema when the Germans were shown retreating towards Berlin, and when an enemy ship went down.

I remember the news item that showed the liberation of the Belsen Concentration Camp and how the entire audience erupted into laughter when the stricken bony frames of the prisoners appeared in what seemed to be *pyjamas*! At the time we none of us knew of the terrible and horrific indignities that had been inflicted and suffered elsewhere in the name of war.

CHAPTER 15

An ever-present column of jade green joined his nose to his upper lip, and to this day I couldn't tell you his true Christian name. To all of us kids at Newfoundland Rd. school he was affectionately known as "Snotty Fox." He lived with his mother and three sisters in a council house near us in Bristol. Snotty's father had just vanished one day some years before. He failed to return home from his job down at the docks and the police were never able to trace him.

Mrs Fox worked at night in the local bakery, then slept most of the morning which meant the kids were on their own for all hours at night and only saw their mum around teatime.

Snotty asked her once if I could come and stay overnight with him and she said yes, very readily. I suppose she was glad to have someone keep him company, because his sisters were all older and involved with other friends and activities.

Snotty was two years older than me and six inches taller. We were all a bit scrawny then, but he was bonier than most of us, and his mended trousers, limp socks and unravelled jersey hung on his frame in a rather divorced manner. Though he sniffed incessantly, he had two very redeeming features. He knew everything there was to know about the more secret aspects of the opposite sex, a knowledge probably attributable to having three sisters, and he could run faster than anyone we knew. It was an ungainly style of movement, though, and his arms held high with elbows out made it difficult to run with him without risking injury.

I t was difficult to run with Snotty Fox without risking personal injury.

As arranged, I went home with him after school on this particular day, and willingly joined in with the round of household tasks. We had to get coal in for the stove that night, and clear out the grate in preparation. We helped Mrs Fox keep the fire going under the copper as she boiled up the washing, and then held on to the heavy wet sheets as she twisted the water out of them and wound them through the mangle. It took all three of us to push up the prop on the clothes line when it was full. Snotty pointed out which knickers belonged to which sister and we stifled giggles in our hands. Joan, the eldest at fourteen, Sarah at twelve and Pat aged eleven, were all busy preparing the tea indoors. The two younger girls were in something of a rush to get off to their "Band of Hope" meeting at St. Paul's church hall.

Tea was bread – of which there was plenty, jam – of which there was little, and cocoa without milk. Mrs Fox went off to her job at the bakery, leaving Snotty and myself and the elder sister Joan to keep the fire in till the others came home again. "Let's go door knockin" said Snotty. "All right" I said, so we tied our scarves round our faces as masks and went out into the damp Bristol streets. This game was new to me, and I didn't really know what was going on when Snotty went up to someone's door and loudly rapped the iron knocker. He then bolted up the street leaving me wondering whether I was supposed to know who answered the door. "Run, run, ya daft bugger!" he screeched, and I left the doorway as the owner appeared. He raged and shook his fist as we rounded the corner. My heart was pounding like a hammer and I thought my eyes would burst, when Snotty, just ahead of me, banged on another door, and with a renewed burst of speed was round the next bend, once again leaving only me in view of the irate old lady who came out.

Snotty pointed out which knickers belonged to which sister.

I was beginning to catch on. "You do the next 'un, Ken" he said. Two streets away from our first door I reached up at a Lion Head knocker, still breathless, when the door opened right in front of me. It was filled by a belly and braces; topped by a red neck and face bursting out of a collarless shirt. I was *thunderstruck*. Snotty was only a patter of diminishing footsteps moving at high speed. "Well, wha's thee want then?" said the face. "Ahh! 'ave you, 'ave you got any odd jobs Mister, I'm collectin' for the Scouts" I said. "I'll gi' thee sixpence to get rid of all these ol' bottles" he said. Within minutes I'd recovered Snotty and my composure, had the bottles tied up in both our overcoats and we were on our way home with thruppence each. From then on the game of door knocking took second place to odd jobbing, it seemed easier on the nerves and better for the pocket.

Snotty was evacuated up to Norfolk when John and I went to Exeter and we gradually drifted apart, but on the few occasions we met up we always laughed over that incident and I think we both learnt something from the experience. The skill of turning an adverse situation to your own advantage is one more common to children than most adults. It certainly added to my store of worldliness that helped me get through childhood relatively unscathed.

CHAPTER 16

My mother, my Gran and Aunty May would take turns holding a place in the food or clothing queues. Some of these were day-long affairs and often entered into without any knowledge of what was being queued for. Places were guarded vigorously, and the only ones permitted to jump the queue were expectant mothers who held a green ration book. I don't think my Gran had a lot of patience with pregnancy used in this way to beat her to the best cuts of meat or the last few tins of pilchards. Those who were classed as "eating for one and a bit" were usually encouraged to take their place at the front with, "C'mon my love, get in yer then" or "Gwan you get up the front my dear." My Gran would grip her basket tightly and mutter "I'd give tuppence to find out if she 'ad a piller up ther" – none the less she gave ground when she had to.

Milk was rationed to two pints a week, and as a result some people took to owning a goat and grazing it in their backyard. Those who could afford the small rent would take an allotment on the edge of the city, and each weekend bend their efforts to growing vegetables. "DIG FOR VICTORY" was a poster seen everywhere. Well, we couldn't afford an allotment, but in very bad times Dennis, Snotty Fox, John and I would go and have a look at the allotments near Durdham Down and give them a bit of a quality test. We weren't very interested in the greens of course, but we regarded ourselves as experienced tasters of carrots and tomatoes. There was the odd occasion when we would pick more tomatoes than we could eat, and then we'd offer the excess to other allotment owners for a reasonable price. Gran was always grudgingly grateful for anything she could add to the week's ration of provisions, and knew just when, and when not, to ask questions.

Up at the allotments there was a shed larger than all the others. Most people had a small building about the size of a phone box to house their gardening tools. This larger shed had a top storey of wire-fronted frames. It was a pigeon loft, and it was owned by a strange old lady with a long grey skirt and a black beret. She always seemed to be up there, seated in the ancient wicker chair outside the loft, cleaning and grooming her pigeons. Now and then she would open the wire frames and release them in a flurry of grain and feathers, and for hours she watched the sky as they circled the loft. Pigeons perched on her head and slightly bent shoulders left us in no doubt that she was probably a loony! But, curiosity being one of the failings of small boys, and with scant regard for what Gran always said it did to the "the cat," all four of us found ourselves up at the allotments one day when the mysterious pigeon lady didn't seem to be around.

Gran and Aunty May listened to our account of the Pigeon Lady at bedtime, then the next morning told us to say nothing more to anyone about her, and to stay away from the allotments. We were a bit surprised at this lack of action, and did in fact keep clear of the allotments for a couple of weeks anyway. When we were next up there we watched the pigeon lady from a distance. Some of her birds flapped in, obviously very exhausted and she caringly dealt with each in turn. She put some inside the hut, and others back in the loft. A black car arrived and took away several baskets placed on the back seat. We were sure then that she was buying and selling black market goods to those who could afford it.

"I'd give tuppence to find out if she 'ad a piller up ther"

At this stage we thought it best to go to a higher authority than Gran and Aunty May, as it was probably more than they could handle. Without delay we set off from the allotments and called in at Ashley Down Police station on the way back. There we gave an account of everything we'd seen over the last few weeks. The officer gave us a good hearing and then called in another man and we had to repeat it over again. They gave us a cup of tea and a big piece of cake, then put us in a police car and drove all four of us back to Monk St.

Once inside, and in front of Gran, the officer explained about the poster we all knew so well which said "Careless Talk Costs Lives." He said we'd done the right thing by going to the police station, but that the pigeon lady was well known to them and she was doing important work for the War Effort. Please forget about it and don't go up there bothering her. This was reinforced by a clip over the ear from Gran when he'd gone. "Why ever can't you mind yer own business when you'm told? Gor bleed'n Imey 'itler don't need an army with you two tykes over 'ere do 'e?"

CHAPTER 17

The men who were considered to be too old for military service were asked to volunteer for the "Local Defence Volunteers." The government hoped to build a home defence made up of a million of these men. They were known as the L.D.V's., but to the ever-joking children they were better known as the Look, Duck and Vanish. They were trained in parade ground drills using sticks instead of rifles, and learnt the art of tank warfare with home-made Molotov Cocktails in lemonade bottles, and they wore denim overalls and a tin hat. Eventually Mr Churchill gave them status and dignity when they were issued with battle-dress uniforms and given the name the Home Guard.

Mr Pym, who ran a sweet and newspaper shop in Pennywell Rd was in charge of a group of these L.D.V's. who regularly paraded in the grounds of Newfoundland Rd school. He was very proud to be doing his bit for the war effort and paraded his men fiercely up and down the playground. The local kids strutted along behind when they marched, and scattered when they about-faced, and now and then a sore bum was earned by a swipe with the broomsticks that took the place of rifles. They were an intrepid band of old guys who spent many nights of fire watching duties, plane spotting and training of all kinds to combat the inevitable German invasion of England.

Raids from the air very often produced the odd dud bomb, which would bury itself some several yards deep on impact, leaving maybe a tail fin just in view at the centre of a large crater. The crater would be roped off and the surrounding area evacuated as soon as possible. The

The local defence volunteers.

U.X.B. (UneXploded Bomb), as it was then known, would be guarded until the bomb disposal squad arrived to defuse and remove it.

Such a bomb hit the ground quite near to Mr Pym's shop one night, and when it was discovered, he was placed in charge of the guard who kept civilians at a safe distance. Mr Pym still had a shop to run, of course, and he presented a comical sight in his denim boiler suit, steel helmet and his mask and his shopkeepers apron, alternately snapping his men to attention while he peered down into the crater, and running into the shop to deal with a customer. My Gran certainly gave him no patience for playing about with "silly bombs" when she wanted a quarter of a pound of fruit gums.

After closing time he was able to devote his time exclusively to the bomb and its crater, and quite proudly invited questions from passers by. The W.V.S. brought the men an evening meal, and while a schedule of guard duty was drawn up Mr Pym selflessly applied himself to assisting the signalman that the regular army had sent to provide communication with a very busy U.X.B. squad currently engaged elsewhere.

After a couple of days the local interest faded somewhat, and there were other raids and emergencies in the meantime. Mr Pym, however, was vigilant! The barrier surrounding the crater became more elaborate, and signs and notices began to appear that made you think it might be an extension of the shop. Arrows pointed to where he might be found in the event of emergency. One sign explained that the bomb was known to be a five hundred pounder high explosive and still dangerous. Mr Pym and other members of the L.D.V's. would sit around an oil stove and brew tea into the night, taking strict turn about to march the perimeter of the protective barricade.

Gran with a basket of ironing.

My Gran took in ironing as an evening job, and when she completed the task she always delivered the basket of pressed clothes back to the owner, no matter what the hour. She harboured a contempt for officialdom that was only surpassed by her contempt for Hitler, and the "bleed'n nuisance" that his war was causing. Mr Pym barricading off Pennywell Rd meant that she would have to walk a considerable distance further to get around the obstacle and complete her delivery. "Not with my feet!!" she vowed, and ducking under the ropes she breasted her basket of ironing down Pennywell Rd and past the unexploded bomb crater.

No amount of "HALT! – Come Back Here!" or "You could be blown up" deterred her as she roared back in like manner and joined in the exchange of rude expletives as she continued on her way. My Aunty May gave her a right telling off when she came home and said what she'd done – Gran was not only surprised at this, she was unrepentant. "If Arthur Pym wants'a put up bits'a rope everybleed'nwhere 'e' can do the sodding ironin'. I ain't buyin' my fruit gums ther' no more neither!"

In the meantime, the impact of the five hundred pounder had broken water and gas mains, which resulted in a sulphurous vapour rising from the crater, and of course the loss of water and gas supply to a large area. The water seepage gradually filled the pit, so that by the time the bomb disposal squad appeared, there was a need for the crater to be pumped out before setting about the job of removal.

We never found out whether the bomb had a time fuse attached or not, but for reasons unknown to us all at the time, it was very much alive and waited almost five days before exploding! It took out a large part of Pennywell Rd, six houses, Mr Pym's shop, and broke windows for a quarter of a mile around. Mr Pym had gone to assist with the transportation of the pumps, and thanks to his vigilance with barricades and evacuation of the surrounding area not one person was injured. When Aunty May read out the details from the paper my Gran never looked up from her ironing.

CHAPTER 18

My Gran always found her tea was too hot to drink from the cup, and having put in the milk and two heaped spoons of jam (there was no sugar) she would then pour the tea into her saucer, and, with a finely balanced spread of the fingers, hold the saucer in one hand. She then proceeded to drink the tea from it. It was a habit that the entire family indulged in on occasions, and one that was typical of working class Britons, at that time. Gran, Aunty May, my Mother, John and I would sit around the scrubbed kitchen table at tea time, eating bread and jam, or a tin of pilchards, and drink the tea from our saucers. Sometimes we had an Oxo cube in hot water instead of tea, or as a special treat, "cocoa."

Towards the end of the war a new drink made its appearance at our table: Camp coffee. This was a thick coffee liquid in what looked like a Worcester sauce bottle. A teaspoonful was carefully poured and then mixed vigorously in your cup of hot water. The milk was in a fat jug, and had also been vigorously mixed as it was powdered milk. We found the baby food dried milk called "Cow N' Gate" was also very suitable for the table. My Gran, along with the help of two working daughters, did her best to provide, but there were occasions when money alone wouldn't buy the food you needed because without the required number of ration coupons to go with the money you simply couldn't make the purchase.

Meat was especially scarce and I don't ever remember having a Sunday roast. There were certainly sausages, and occasionally chops, but never, never, steak... We sometimes ate rabbit, for special occasions, though you could never get that song out of your mind while you were eating them. Liver, kidneys and sheep's hearts sometimes appeared on the table, and my Gran was a wizard with chitlings or faggots and peas. Other meals were provided at the local fish and chip shop in Pennywell Rd. Variety in those times was not really a problem, but the quality may have been more questionable. It was no surprise to see a large pot boiling on the wood stove one cold September evening, already dark as we came in from school. Mum and Aunty May wouldn't arrive home from work before 7 p.m. and the evening meal wasn't served until we were all in. "Wha's fer tea Gran?" our John said. "Ne'er mind! – thee just better eat and be grateful" she snapped.

John and I went out the back to play in the Anderson shelter on the pretext of tidying it up, and of course to pull one or three life sustaining carrots from the garden on top of it. It was a long time before tea. We hoisted Dennis in over a side fence in a prearranged plan, because as two brothers we couldn't play satisfactorily on our own. We then set up house in the shelter by lighting the emergency candles with the never-to-be-used matches, and sat around discussing the day's events.

Through crunchy carrots we condemned Beryl Bates because we were sure she had nits. She was always scratching her head, and when you teased her she came and shook her hair all over you – dirty monkey! Pearl Jones showed her bloomers in the playground doing handstands and Miss Fisk told her off good and proper. Did Miss Fisk wear a wig? It was a strong rumour round Newfoundland Rd. school.

When Gran summoned us for tea with a "C'mon you two tykes!!" we blew out the stubs of candle and hoisted Dennis back over the fence. When we bounded back into the kitchen it was to find Mum and Aunty May already at the table. Gran lifted the steaming pot off the hob and, centring it on the table she began to ladle the green mixture she had prepared into bowls.

"Wha's that then Mother?" inquired Aunty May as she craned forward. "Never thee mind" said Gran. We all sniffed at the steam and probed at the jelly-like meat pieces that floated in our bowls. Without further question (for we all knew better) we set to, and Mum launched into an account of her day's work. The rest of the evening passed without incident.

It was about a month later that the same mixture appeared on the stove again. John and I were home from evacuation billets and anxious to please so we wouldn't get sent away again. We arrived home straight from school to see if we could help Gran and she was busying herself in the garden. "Go on then" she said, "Get theeself a jar an' help me get these off." She was removing the snails from a large patch of lilies that grew beyond the clothes line. Within ten minutes we had filled three large jars. "Give em yer" she said, and she took them into the greenhouse where she filled the jars with vinegar. This made the snails fizz like sherbet all over the place, and it also made them leave their shells. She then washed them in cold water and tipped them into the boiling pot on the stove.

At some time or other the information must have filtered down through the classes that a great food delicacy was enjoyed on the Continent in the form of snails, and though we as children didn't question it, my Aunty May that night voiced her opinion. Gran looked very hard at her across the table, daring her to say more. Then as she ladled the mixture into bowls she said, "If its good enough for them Frenchies, it'll do you my gurl."

CHAPTER 19

When you lived a "sheltered life," what was uplifting was a pro-gramme which we heard every week on the radio called *Into Battle*. It always started with the *Lilliburlero*. It was terrific, a really stirring tune and then they would tell you of an incident in one man's war for that week, like a parachutist who was shot out of his plane, his parachute burning. He came down in a small village in France and eight Germans tried to capture him – nevertheless he killed them all and was spirited back to England by the French Underground.

I suppose less than half the stories you were told were true. The prop-aganda machine was in operation to keep the spirits up, and it generally worked – except when you had a raid where the whole district would be shattered and the people demoralised, and you were told on the news how minor the damage had been and that a great number of enemy planes had been shot down. None of it true! Repeated doses of this con-tributed to Churchill losing office in 1945, I believe. There were major mistakes made at times, many of which were only revealed in hushed tones, or in fact were not revealed until well after the war ended.

There was the parachutist who bailed out of his stricken plane and landed in farmland up in the north of England. His broken English gave him no credibility with the local farmers, who proceeded to beat him to death with picks and staves. He turned out to be a Polish airman flying with the R.A.F. Then there was the Canadian force shot to pieces with live rounds that were supposed to be blanks during a beach landing exercise on the south coast. Fifty-one died in that mistake.

There were the evacuees and escorts who were enroute to safety in the United States aboard the "City of Benares." Aboard were some three hundred people. They were torpedoed in the mid-Atlantic, and two hundred and sixty of them perished, of whom eighty-four were children. The "City of Benares" had on board Colonel J. Baldwin Webb, who was heading for the United States to urge the American government to enter the war on the side of the British. He was in the company of the German refugee Rudolph Olden who was going to America for the same purpose. Just the presence of these two men aboard the "City of Benares" made her anything but a mercy ship. Further to that, the Germans argued that the ship was assigned to bring back a large cargo of war supplies from Canada and the United States.

At home in places like Bristol, Liverpool and Southampton there would be a major exodus from the city between the hours of six and eight heading for the country away from target areas like the docks, and then returning in time to go back to work in the morning. This attempt to avoid being bombed in your home often resulted in your home being stripped overnight by looters. Human nature didn't change because there was a war on! There was a very large-scale operation in London that even used field telephone communications to co-ordinate trucks that loaded up looted goods while the owners were sheltering down in the Tube stations. Shops, factories and private homes all suffered losses on the home front which were not always instigated by the Germans. "Makes you wonder oo the bleed'n enemy is" my Gran would say.

The C.O.R.B. or Childrens Overseas Reception Board brought English evacuees to other English speaking countries around the world for safety – places as far afield as South Africa, Rhodesia, Australia and

New Zealand. Some interesting details are contained in the C.O.R.B. files, which have only been made available for research since 1980. For example, the Dominions let it be known that they wanted a balanced migration, a cross-section of British life that represented both rich and poor classes. The only requests for "Pure Stock" came from the United States. The British government passed a strict law forbidding all people aged from sixteen to sixty to leave the country, unless they were chosen as escorts on the ships transporting the children. Churchill was very much against large scale evacuation from England as it gave "Comfort to the Enemy" he said. *Dunkirk* and all that it implied speeded up the process and in September 1940 the S.S Ruahine steamed for New Zealand with a precious cargo of children, mostly from Scotland. The "Rangitata" and the "Rangitane" were other ships of the New Zealand Shipping Line to be involved in this programme eventually, and the ill-fated Rangitane was sunk by a German raider just four days out of Auckland on Wednesday the 27th November 1940. Three raiders, two of them flying Japanese flags, opened fire on the Rangitane at 3.30 a.m. on that day. She was carrying a number of adult escorts who had accompanied evacuee children out to New Zealand. Six of these were killed in the initial attack and the survivors eventually were picked up by the "Leander," a New Zealand naval vessel, from a tiny desert island named Emirau off New Guinea, where they had been abandoned.

These tragic affairs serve to illustrate that major errors of judgement proliferated throughout the war years with disastrous consequences. For those that affected children, the trauma continues on into their adult lives. Evacuees are noted for their emotional reserve born of an unwillingness to trust.

CHAPTER 20

Suddenly, Dennis Jay and Snotty Fox appeared back in Bristol and though we hadn't seen them for many months, we picked up again as a gang right where we'd left off.

I'm sure it can now be told because the shop we all knew as "The Don" in Newfoundland Rd. has long been demolished and so has Monk St. and I always knew that some day we would have to confess. It was Dennis Jay and myself that perpetrated the crime of robbery on this "Aladdin's Cave" of comics, sherbets, liquorice and small change. Dennis, like me, was small, grubby, impoverished and always ready to accept "A Dare" and it came about by chance as we were playing on the coal pile in Scapens backyard.

Climbing to the top of the newly dumped coal that was used to warm and brighten the lives of the pub customers, we discovered that we overlooked the back of the shop known as "The Don." As the coal heap mounted the back wall, it was only a drop to the ground on the other side and we were just yards from the shop's backdoor. The louvre window beside this opened easily, and in a matter of seconds we were inside a small store room.

Beyond a curtained doorway the shop itself was bathed in a greenish glow from the gas street-lamp that shone through the window. Dennis was a tactician and not of an impetuous nature. "Tell you what," he said, "I'll go out the front door so I can keep watch, and you can shove the stuff out through the letter-box." His gappy teeth showed clearly in the strange light as he set his lips firmly. Pausing only to fill

"Hey Ken... 'member that time we robbed the 'The Don'?"

his mouth with wine gums that were in an open box on the counter, he undid the main door bolts and slid out of view.

I looked around in the green enhancement of the early evening gloom. Stepping cautiously behind the counter, I ran childish fingers along the rows of jars and the toffee tins. Lifting selected ones down it soon became apparent that most of them were empty and only serving to fill the shelves so I turned my attention to the counter: wine gums, yeah! – in the pocket. Sherbet dabs? – no time for that, and too messy. I pulled open a drawer in the counter and was startled by a loud DING!

Dennis appeared at the main window somewhat agitated and, cupping his face in his hands he called, "Wot bist doin in ther? Lock the bleed'n door case anyone comes." I moved quickly to the door and secured the bolts then lifted the letter slot. "Ay Dennis, thers money in that drawer." "Well, poke it thru ere," he said, "I'll catch it in me cap."

The chocolate box inside the drawer contained pennies, ha'pennies and farthings. I scooped as many as two hands would hold and began feeding them through the letter slot. Dennis was giggling and we both enjoyed a sense of elation at the continued sound of coins clinking into his cap. I went back for more. Dennis remarked that we could come back in the morning and spend it – that seemed like a good idea! Coins of the realm continued to mount in Dennis's cap for several minutes and then, I noticed a change in the sound. Some coins now seemed to be hitting the pavement. I pulled up the letter slot and called, "Wos 'appened? Your cap full?" No reply. "Dennis!" I peered out through the slot where my vision was now blocked by a vast expanse of blue serge – then the contorted face of Dennis came into view, his ear pinched between a copper's fingers.

It was a moment of indescribable terror, not so much fear of the policeman but the thought that he would tell Mum and my Gran. We had to put the money back of course and then show him how we got in. He wrote everything down in his book. At the end of the ordeal we were very sorry boys, and went off home full of foreboding about the consequences of it all. Nothing happened! Dennis and I would meet and whisper urgently about it, we even avoided going into the 'The Don' in case our guilt showed.

It may or may not have been his intention but I can tell you that the protracted time over which we expected punishment that never happened caused a change in our behaviour pattern which lasted much longer than the usual recriminations would have achieved.

I came across Dennis Jay when I returned to Bristol for a visit in 1956 and as he approached me on the street he said, "Oh! 'ello Ken I amt seen you in a while, you 'ad the flu?" Ten years had elapsed.

Dennis and Snotty had both been evacuated up to Norfolk and by all accounts had a pretty good time on farms up there. Certainly never heard an angry shot or a bomb. Snotty continued to be well-named as he still displayed the candles on his nose, and perhaps that was the reason behind his story. It seemed that the group of single evacuees (that is, without brothers or sisters) arrived at the village where they were to be billeted, and were ushered into the local hall. The W.V.S. and the local villagers set about trying to place each one and we remembered our own experience in Cheddar as Snotty described how the clean, angel-faced ones were snapped up, and the embarrassing hesitation before he was escorted away last of all. Dennis was placed on a neighbouring farm and they went to school together, though they never felt the need to run away and head for home.

It was good to be all back together again and to roam the streets, accosting the Yanks with "Got any gum chum?" – they had a free issue and they usually obliged. Many of the servicemen we saw now were the wounded who had been released from hospitals, perhaps limping on sticks or wheelchair bound. One told of having a plate in his head! but I couldn't see how that could be cos surely the shape of a plate would show – like wearing a tin helmet all the time. Some of them shook and twitched all the time and you couldn't get any conversation from them at all. Mum said they were shell-shocked and would be all right in time.

The drone of flights of heavy bombers, and the sight of dogfights with Spitfires and Focke Wolfs over Durdham Down had been finished for some time, and the bowel-watering sound of the air raid siren was hardly heard. All the closeted activities of the city began to re-emerge. Railway station signs and street names were put back up. The sticking plaster on windows to avoid damage from flying glass was removed and you could have lights on at night without using blackout blinds.

Most important to the kids was that you were allowed out into the fields once again. The barbed wire was removed from the open spaces where it had been placed to prevent landings, and once more we had access to the good scrumping places. "Scrumping" was the word given to the raiding of orchards for apples, pears or other fruits and we were quick to return to our favourite scrumping place out at Hortham. The corporation swimming baths were only mildly damaged in the blitz and were soon re-opened. Though John and I couldn't swim we enjoyed being there, and we would wet our woollen knitted swimming costumes in the pool to show Mum we were trying.

Apple scrumping!

Activities on the bomb sites too gave us hours of adventure, and we were only mildly deterred when we heard of the deaths of two kids who tried to unearth an unexploded bomb from the rubble. The U.X.B. Squads were busy for many months on this menace. Dennis Jay's father had been in the R.A.F. and he took us all out to Filton Aerodrome, which was a huge air base not far out of Bristol city, and we were able to see inside a Wellington Bomber. Little did we know that a year from then we'd be living in a place of that name on the other side of the world.

CHAPTER 21

A big map of Europe in the window of "The Don" showed that the Germans were being rapidly driven back to Berlin, and each morning everyone would gather outside "The Don" to wring hands and jump up and down with glee as the little British and American flags were moved forward, narrowing the gap on the Russians who held firm on the other side of the German city. We all made Guy Fawkes type images of Hitler and Goering, and started to collect rubbish for a big bonfire celebration because it now seemed only a matter of time.

Mum and John and me were in the fold-out sofa bed at 79 Ashley Rd. Bristol when the news came that Hitler was dead and the Germans had surrendered. All the windows in the road shot up and people were shouting to each other and hanging their radios out of the windows in case someone hadn't heard. You just had to get up and go out into the streets. I think everyone in Bristol made for the Centre that night because you couldn't move in the crowd. John and I got up on the roof of an air raid shelter, and although we weren't alone we got quickly to a Grand Circle position by running over their flat tops and jumping the narrow gaps between them, Uniforms of all kinds were dancing and kissing and carrying each other shoulder high, no-one wore their own hat and there was a bottle in every spare hand.

We burnt our bonfires and threw Hitler on when the heat was fiercest and we sang "Land of Hope and Glory" through tears brought on by the bonfire and the sheer relief of having survived. "Bout bleed'n time too!" was my Gran's reaction to the news of V.E. Day. It seemed a very short time later that the Japanese surrendered too and we were greatly

79 Ashley Road.

surprised to hear that they'd given up after only *two* bombs had been dropped on them.

I remember John and I having our first haircuts in a real barber shop as a special treat at the end of the war; up to then it had always been a scissors cut round any hair that poked out from under a pudding basin on your head. Mum had another reason for making us look our best too: she was anxious for us to meet her new husband Jack. He was in the New Zealand Navy and he was going to take us all for a seaside holiday at Weymouth. He was a big and very hairy man with a wide grin of sparkling white teeth.

The Weymouth holiday never happened, though, because Jack returned to ship hurriedly and she set sail for New Zealand for a thing called being "demobbed", and that brief meeting with him was the only time I ever saw him. Jack was off-loaded at Colombo in Ceylon and there he died of smallpox in 1945, leaving my mother as an official war bride. So, once again a widow with the sad death of her husband of only eleven weeks my mother made the decision which was to change all our lives. As we were eligible for assisted passage we were going to move to a place called Wellington in New Zealand to live with Jack's mother, Eileen.

I remember having very mixed feelings about this at the time. After all, we had only just finished what seemed to be a four year exercise in the game of "Find Your Way Home" and each time we seemed to be sent further and further away from Bristol to make it harder. Now we were all back together and the war was finished. Mind you it wouldn't be as bad as being evacuated because Mum would be going with us this time. But twelve thousand miles seemed a bit much. I did a kind of silent pilgrimage around all the places I knew saying to myself, "this is the last time I'll see this" or "this is the last time I'll do this." As it happened it wasn't, but as I gave my Gran and Aunty May a tearful hug and kiss the thought was there, and it proved to be right. The two most loving and warm sanctuaries of my family were to die within months of each other in 1951. Dennis Jay gave me a dagger sheath knife in a scabbard and he gave John a wallet and we all said a tearful good-bye at Temple Meads Station as we took the train to London.

The New Zealand Line ship *"Rangitiki"* was the biggest ship I'd ever seen and she was black with two yellow funnels. Mum, John and I shared a cabin with one other family and we left Tilbury docks on February 6th 1946. The entire shipload of passengers was made up of War Brides and their children, some bound for Australia and others for New Zealand. After some early seasickness that everybody fell victim to, we settled into a happy and well- fed voyage that lasted six weeks.

It wasn't without incident, either, as we came by way of recently ravaged shipping lanes of the Atlantic to turn left at Gibraltar into the Mediterranean. We passed a mine or two gently bobbing their way a couple of hundred yards off our beam – and these were only the ones we actually saw! We all cheerfully lined up on deck in our swimming costumes for a salt water hosing that knocked you off your feet, and there were free ice creams brought round on trays by stewards at three o'clock. It all seemed a bit like one of those Hollywood luxury movies. I wouldn't have been a bit surprised if Bud Abbott and Lou Costello had been serving at the tables, or if Bob Hope had come down among us as the Captain. There were lots of games, parties, organised dances and fancy dress events. Tennis, quoits, horse racing, skittles – in fact a whole host of activities to keep you amused and healthy.

We stopped briefly at Gibraltar and then at Malta before taking our turn through the Suez Canal. It was all so wonderful and exotic to pass pyramids and camel trains and to actually be where so many exciting Champion Comic stories had been spawned. At Port Said, the ship anchored offshore but was soon surrounded by swimming Egyptians asking for coins to be thrown into the sea so they could dive for them. It seemed a reasonable request to throw only the white ones because the brown ones were hard to see in the murky water, until I realised that I was only holding pennies and ha'pennies after throwing a shilling and several sixpences into the briny! The boats that came alongside did enormous trade in leather wallets and handbags. The goods were transported up to the ship's rail with an ingenious system of rope and basket on a running loop. The basket would bring the goods up for inspection and take the money down to the bobbing traders.

It was here in Port Said that someone gave me a banana. I had never seen them before and had no idea how to eat it, until I was shown the method of peeling them. We seemed to strike bottom several times while enroute through the canal but the crew said it was quite usual so we didn't worry. We called in at Aden and then began the long cruise across to Ceylon at the foot of India. We basked in the long sunshine hours and browned our very white bodies, while we drank tall cool fruit juice drinks. Life was just wonderful. Every now and then we threw ourselves into the discipline of lifeboat drill. We donned fore and aft life jackets and ran to boat stations, and in fact became very competitive over it. After all, we had just come from a long term of drills and disciplines to shouts, whistles and sirens – was there any other way of life?

On arrival in Ceylon, Mum was allowed ashore under escort in order to visit Jack's grave and I think she was the only one to leave the ship during the entire voyage. I told everyone that the only reason we were stopping at Ceylon was for my Mum!

A few days out from Ceylon some of the ship's crew were asking the question – "Did you feel the bump in the night?" Nobody had, of course, but it was the seaman's way of telling you that you had crossed the line of the equator. A great celebration was held on deck and King Neptune was hauled up over the side. He proceeded to lather and shave selected members of the passengers and crew with a gigantic bucket of foamy suds and a wooden cut-throat razor. People were plastered with flour and water glue and then hosed down, and all who were aboard received a certificate for crossing the line and were declared "Pollywogs of the Sea."

We next saw land at Fremantle, and there we said good-bye to a large group of war brides and kids about to make a new life in Australia, and after doing the same at Melbourne the ship seemed rather empty.

A sudden change in the weather kept us all in cabins for the next four days but on the morning of the fifth day it dawned beautifully fine and we were all on deck to slowly round the Heads of Wellington Harbour. It was 7.30 a.m. on March 28th 1946 when I first saw the doll's houses scattered about the hills of the capital city of New Zealand, and each and every one seemed to have a red iron roof. By 1 o'clock that day we were sitting down to a salad lunch, so I was told – the only meals I knew were breakfast, dinner and tea; and I could look out the window at a building called the *Freelance* from our new home at 33 The Terrace.

It's natural that exevacuees should feel the need to revisit places to which they were evacuated. There are many who look back upon happy times, and such visits are sweetly nostalgic. There are those who make the pilgrimage in the hope that a return to the scene might repair some of the psychological damage and enable them to live the rest of their lives in peace.

For my part, the years have diminished the pain to an emotional memory recall, and that pain is the pain of separation, not of any ill treatment. A confusion persists though, as to what constitutes a full and rewarding childhood. Because in spite of the dangers and privations, mine was one Great Adventure. Tears that I may not have shed as a child found an embarrassingly full flow in the archives of Exeter Library during a visit in September 1992. Among a very large pile of evacuation material, I found a brown file card which they allowed me to photocopy:

Householder: DAWSON, E., Mrs.					No.: 24979	
Address: 19 Kater Lane, EXETER					EXETER	
Accommodation:			Remarks:		Ward Reference:	
Name of Evacuee	Age	Date of Billeting	No. of Order	Weekly Amount	Transfers, etc.	
Beachem, John (B)	8	1943 Apr. 28th.	BB. 3434	12/-		
Beachem, Kenneth	7			10/-		

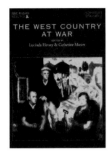